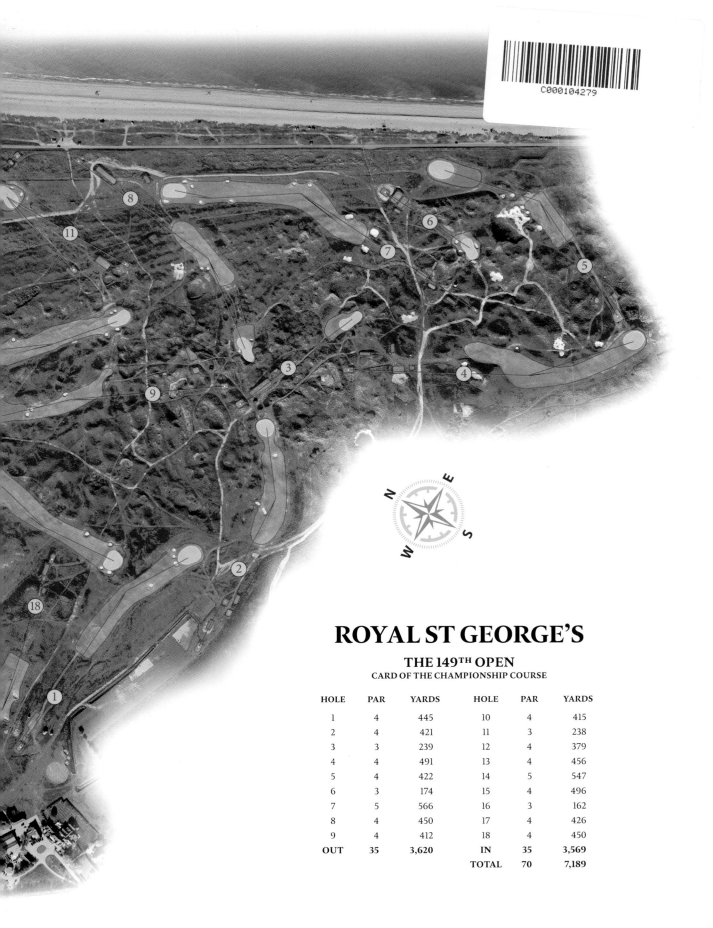

ROYAL ST GEORGE'S

THE 149TH OPEN
CARD OF THE CHAMPIONSHIP COURSE

HOLE	PAR	YARDS	HOLE	PAR	YARDS
1	4	445	10	4	415
2	4	421	11	3	238
3	3	239	12	4	379
4	4	491	13	4	456
5	4	422	14	5	547
6	3	174	15	4	496
7	5	566	16	3	162
8	4	450	17	4	426
9	4	412	18	4	450
OUT	35	3,620	IN	35	3,569
			TOTAL	70	7,189

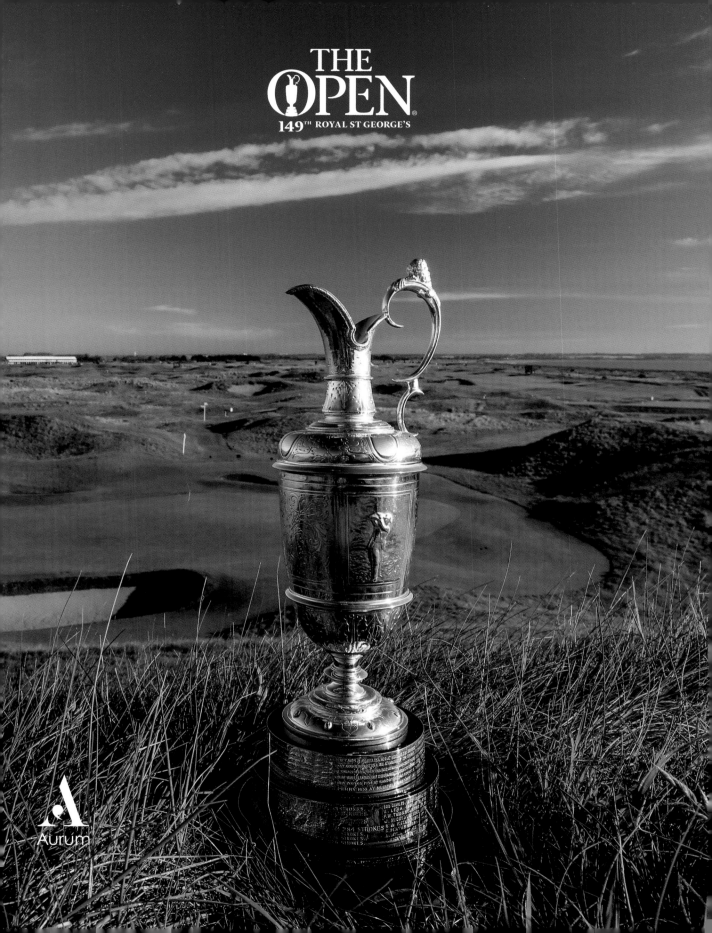

R&A

Aurum Press
74-77 White Lion Street, London N1 9PF

Published 2021 by Aurum Press

Copyright 2021 R&A Championships Limited

Course aerial © Bluesky International Limited

Project coordinator: Sarah Wooldridge
Additional thanks to:
SMT – SportsMEDIA Technology
Peter Kollmann
Rob Harborne

A CIP catalogue record for this book is available
from the British Library

ISBN 978-0-71127-447-1

Designed and produced by TC Communications Ltd
Printed in Italy by L.E.G.O.

EDITOR
Andy Farrell

WRITERS AND PHOTOGRAPHERS

Writers	The R&A	Getty Images	R&A Photo Editors
Peter Dixon	David Cannon	Andrew Redington	Kate McShane
John Hopkins	Warren Little	Chris Trotman	Joe Perch
Lewine Mair	Matt Lewis	Mike Hewitt	Paul Harding
Art Spander	Charlie Crowhurst	Christopher Lee	
Alistair Tait	Harry Trump	Oisin Keniry	
	Tom Shaw		
	Stephen Pond		

Foreword

By Collin Morikawa

"Chills." That's how I described hearing my name announced as the Champion Golfer of the Year and I still have them. Closing it out to win The 149th Open was one of the best moments of my life. I will remember it forever. The Claret Jug is amazing. To etch my name on it, along with countless Hall of Famers and people I have looked up to, is so special.

It is hard to look back on the two short years I have been a professional and see what I've achieved because I want more. I truly love what I do, competing for the biggest prizes in the game against the best players in the world. I have to give credit to a big team that supports me — they don't get it enough — including my family, my girlfriend Kat, my coach, agent, sponsors, and my caddie, JJ Jakovac — it was fun getting the fans at the 18th green to sing him "Happy Birthday".

This was my first time at The Open and it was an amazing experience. Thank you to Royal St George's Golf Club and The R&A for the opportunity to play on such a phenomenal stage and for keeping us safe. And a huge thank you to the fans. They are some of the best I've ever seen. They truly understand the game and, with the energy they provide cheering us on, it was so much fun playing in front of them.

I look forward to defending my title at St Andrews next year. The Open Championship is going to be part of my life for the rest of my life no matter what happens. To be a part of that history, it's awesome.

The R&A
Open Championships Committee

CHAIRMAN
David C Meacher

DEPUTY CHAIR
Anne O'Sullivan

COMMITTEE
Áine Binchy
Tim Cockroft
Gavin Lawrie
Hans Lindeblad
Alastair Wells

CHIEF EXECUTIVE
Martin Slumbers

EXECUTIVE DIRECTOR – CHAMPIONSHIPS
Johnnie Cole-Hamilton

EXECUTIVE DIRECTOR – GOVERNANCE
David Rickman

Introduction

By David C Meacher, Chairman, Open Championships Committee

The 149th Open at Royal St George's will be remembered for a record-breaking performance on his first appearance in the Championship by Collin Morikawa, who lifted the famous Claret Jug after a two-shot victory over Jordan Spieth.

On his way to becoming the 2021 Champion Golfer of the Year, Morikawa created a new record for four rounds in The Open at Royal St George's after finishing on a 15-under-par total of 265, beating the previous best set by Greg Norman in 1993 by two shots.

In many ways this was an Open like no other. Played during a global pandemic that has affected so many people's lives, we staged a safe and secure Championship that was enjoyed in glorious weather by over 150,000 fans who generated a very special atmosphere.

We were able to do this as part of the UK Government's Events Research Programme and I would like to thank the UK government and public health authorities for their invaluable support in making the Championship possible this year. The staff of The R&A also deserve enormous credit for their dedication, expertise and commitment in delivering all aspects of the Championship to the highest standards. I would also like to thank the members and staff of Royal St George's Golf Club for their partnership and the support and hard work that went into delivering a world class course that challenged the very best men's professional golfers. They have also shown remarkable patience and resilience in the face of having to host the Championship in very different circumstances.

We have thousands of volunteers who work tirelessly before and during the Championship to ensure its smooth running and we are very grateful for their hard work and commitment. I also wish to thank the local agencies in Kent who have provided vital support and guidance in helping to stage another successful Championship.

We now look forward to a historic occasion next year when The 150th Open is played at St Andrews and welcoming fans to the Home of Golf for what will be a memorable celebration of golf's original Championship.

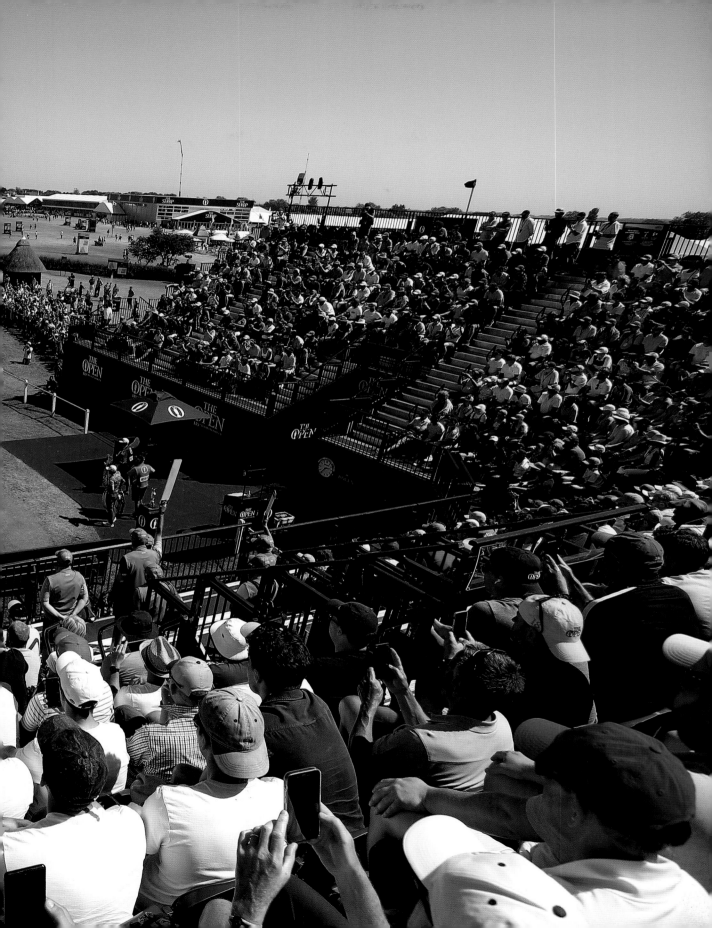

WELCOME TO
THE
OPEN

THE VENUE

Stranger Than Fiction

By Andy Farrell

As a stage for great players and great championships, Royal St George's has seen it all. Triumph and disaster, history and drama, incidents and accidents, all set among ancient sand dunes that saw Julius Caesar and Emperor Claudius pass by two millennia ago and have been shaped by vast extremes of weather for even longer.

It is not just golfers who have been inspired by the setting. Authors, too. Bernard Darwin, one of the finest golf writers, was a long-term president of the club, while novelist Ian Fleming was captain-elect when he died of a heart attack in 1964. Both wrote fictional accounts of matches at St George's.

Sorting fact from fiction goes all the way back to the origins of the club. The story goes that a London ophthalmologist, Dr William Laidlaw Purves, a Scot who was fed up of the muddy and crowded courses set on commons at Wimbledon and Blackheath, scoured the south coast from Dorset to Kent before discovering the best land on which to lay the sort of links offered by his homeland.

It appears that the "lengthy investigation and many days of travel" may have been the good doctor gilding the lily. The club's own official history provides evidence that it was his brother, Alex, who suggested a trip to Sandwich since he was interested in the archaeology connected to the Roman invasions. The top of the tower of St Clement's church was a good place to start. "By George," exclaimed the golfing doctor, "what a place for a golf course!"

Or three. The game had been played on the dunes in a limited way for a while, but soon there were three first-rate clubs that all became hosts of The Open.

The sun rises over Royal St George's for The 149th Open.

St George's was the first, founded by Laidlaw Purves and two fellow Wimbledon Scots in 1887, to be followed by Cinque Ports to the south, on the outskirts of Deal, and Prince's to the north, so close that Mr Polwinkle, the hero in Darwin's short story, *The Wooden Putter*, goes to sleep dreaming of "mashie shots with so much backspin on them that they pitched on Prince's and came back into the hole on St George's."

But who needs fiction when much of the venue's folklore is of the couldn't-make-it-up variety. When Walter Hagen won the first of two Opens at Sandwich in 1922, he was an early finisher and the London evening papers proclaiming his victory were being sold on the course as George Duncan made a late charge. But the Scot missed out on a play-off when he took three to get down from the dip on the left of the 18th green ever after called "Duncan's Hollow". Sandy Lyle, on his knees, thumped the turf when his ball rolled back to his feet in the same spot but he ended up a relieved Champion Golfer in 1985.

Indigestion, perhaps from a rogue lunchtime sandwich, almost derailed Henry Cotton in 1934 as he closed with a 79, but his lead had been so commanding he still became the first home winner for over a decade. Reg Whitcombe battled to a 78 to win four years later in a gale so severe that the exhibition tent was lost out to sea and Alf Padgham drove the green at the then 384-yard 11th hole, and made a 2, but was still short at the 14th after hitting his driver four times.

In 1949, Harry Bradshaw played a shot with his ball nestling in a broken glass bottle and survived to tell the tale, eventually losing a play-off to Bobby Locke. The Rules of Golf were later clarified to state a player in such a situation was entitled to a free drop.

Spectators throng the Maiden behind the sixth green; once upon a time, players faced a blind shot over the top of it.

A marshal stands atop the huge Himalayas bunker at the fourth hole; it was recently renovated for a more natural look.

Perfect summer weather to be beside the sea down by the tees for the eighth and 12ᵗʰ holes.

Bill Rogers, the 1981 Champion Golfer, almost missed his tee time on the first day after misreading the starting sheet and was only saved by a journalist who spotted the American on the putting green just in time. Three St George's Opens later, in 2003, Mark Roe was disqualified for signing for a wrong score — he was right in contention in the third round — when he and Jesper Parnevik failed to swap scorecards.

That was the year Tiger Woods lost a ball on his opening tee shot and Thomas Bjorn took three to get out of the bunker at the short 16th. Ben Curtis won on his debut having been the first player to arrive and the only one to spend time talking to the club professional at the time, Andrew Brooks, on how to play the course. Remarkably, for a links that is supposed to take much local knowledge and appreciation for the shifting winds off Pegwell Bay, the last two Champions to win on their Open debuts, including Collin Morikawa, came here.

Players have been complaining about blind shots at St George's all the way back to the days of the great amateur Freddie Tait. Laidlaw Purves laid out the original course in the "sporty" fashion of the time — long carries off the tees, blind shots over the dunes. It did not take long for The Open to visit, in 1894,

the first time it had been staged outside Scotland. It helped that JH Taylor and Harry Vardon, two-thirds of the Great Triumvirate, won the first two Opens at St George's.

It has always been a course to inspire excellence from great players, as Morikawa showed in his two-stroke victory in 2021. When Vardon won again at Sandwich in 1911, he defeated Arnaud Massy, the 1907 Champion Golfer, so comprehensively in the play-off that the Frenchman was left lamenting, "I cannot play this damn game."

Having seen his American opponent Don Moe recover from seven down with 13 to play to win a Walker Cup singles at the 36th with a 3-iron to three feet, a stunned Bill Stout said afterwards, "That wasn't golf, Don, that was a visitation from the Lord." Cotton's 65 in the second round in 1934, a new record for The Open, was celebrated in the title of a bestselling golf ball, the "Dunlop 65". And when Greg Norman won The Open in 1993 with a final round of 64, Gene Sarazen, winner of The Open at Prince's in 1932, declared, "I never thought I'd live to see golf played so well."

Could anything in fiction live up to all that? Well, Mr Polwinkle, inspired to play in the manner of the

greats whose clubs he has collected over the years, gives it a go. At the first hole, in common with modern Open competitors but not most golfers of the 1920s, he hits his Braid driver "far over the 'Kitchen', that grassy hollow that has caught and stopped so many hundreds of balls."

While the course has been fine-tuned many times over the decades, removing blind shots, moving bunkers, widening fairways, the essence of the course remains from Darwin's 1928 short story and Fleming's 1959 novel, *Goldfinger.* Perhaps Morikawa and Oosthuizen, Spieth and Rahm, walked off the first tee and, as James Bond, "smelled the sweet smell of the beginning of a knock-down-and-drag-out game of golf on a beautiful day with the larks singing over the greatest seaside course in the world."

Darwin writes of the second hole: "As all the world knows, there is a long and joyous carry from the tee. A really fine shot will soar over the bunker and the hilltop beyond, and the ball will lie in a little green valley, to be pitched home onto the green."

Fleming of the fourth: "You drive over one of the tallest and deepest bunkers in the United Kingdom and then have a long second shot across an undulating, hilly

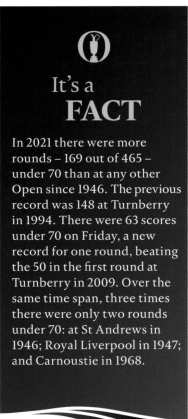

It's a
FACT

In 2021 there were more rounds – 169 out of 465 – under 70 than at any other Open since 1946. The previous record was 148 at Turnberry in 1994. There were 63 scores under 70 on Friday, a new record for one round, beating the 50 in the first round at Turnberry in 2009. Over the same time span, three times there were only two rounds under 70: at St Andrews in 1946; Royal Liverpool in 1947; and Carnoustie in 1968.

Beware the ever shifting winds off Pegwell Bay between Sandwich and Ramsgate.

Ready for The 149th Open: Royal St George's formidable 18th hole in its natural guise in July 2020

A favourable links all round

It was not just the world's greatest golfers on show during The 149th Open but some of the rarest wild orchids found in the country.

Not merely content with overseeing the presentation of a sustainable golf course with the finest seaside fescues on the tees, fairways and greens, as well as natural-looking bunkers, Paul Larsen, the head greenkeeper at Royal St George's, has also been managing the whole dune system to such good effect that the area has gained favourable status as a Site of Special Scientific Interest.

"This is the highest you can be and is something I and the club are very proud of," Larsen said. "It really highlights our sustainability to the dunes, plus it proves that golf courses can be an asset to the natural land. We work in partnership with all our environmental friends to maintain the best practice for the dunes.

"We don't water the rough as it needs to remain natural and 'wispy'. By maintaining low water levels on these areas they have a better chance of retaining fescue, sweet vernal, crested dogs-tail, bedstraw, broom rape and lizard orchid."

Larsen stopped mowing large areas between tees and fairways, while problem spots of non-native grasses were burnt off. "It is incredible to see as everything burns out apart from little strands of marram. It is completely black and desolate for about six weeks, but then you see it come back to life. You lose that lush thickness, but regain the marram, plus we have never seen so many wild flowers on the course, with a massive increase in lizard orchids."

For the first time, The Open featured a Sustainability Zone showing off the latest low-carbon technologies. Continuing their initiative from 2019 of eliminating single-use plastic water bottles, The R&A also introduced an electric fleet of Mercedes-Benz courtesy cars and utilised Aggreko biodiesel generators, as well as solar power, for The 149th Open.

ROYAL ST GEORGE'S CHAMPIONS

1894	JH Taylor
1899	Harry Vardon
1904	Jack White
1911	Harry Vardon
1922	Walter Hagen
1928	Walter Hagen
1934	Henry Cotton
1938	Reg Whitcombe
1949	Bobby Locke
1981	Bill Rogers
1985	Sandy Lyle
1993	Greg Norman
2003	Ben Curtis
2011	Darren Clarke
2021	Collin Morikawa

For the first time the Sustainability Zone featured in the Tented Village.

fairway to a plateau green guarded by a final steep slope which makes it easier to take three putts than two."

At the fifth, "Bond stood on the tee, perched high up in the sand-hills, and paused before the shot while he gazed at the glittering distant sea and at the faraway crescent of white cliffs beyond Pegwell Bay. Then he took up his stance and visualised the tennis court of turf that was his target."

That the sixth hole no longer played over the highest dune on the site still rankled with Darwin, as his protagonist makes clear, bemoaning that they "do not now play over the Maiden's crown, but only over the lower spurs — touching, as it were, but the skirts of her sandy garment."

Of the 10th hole, Darwin points out the need to avoid "that horrid, trappy bunker that waits voraciously at the left-hand corner of the plateau green." Fleming agrees it is the "most dangerous hole on the course. The second shot, to the skinny plateau green with cavernous bunkers to right and left and a steep hill beyond, has broken many hearts."

The drive at the 14th hole, running along the boundary with Prince's, concentrates Bond's mind with "out of bounds over the fence on the right and the drive into the breeze favouring a slice!" Bernhard

Langer and Dustin Johnson are among those to have fallen victim in the past, and Robert MacIntyre and Marcel Siem among those in 2021.

Bond has more to deal with than just the course — which is given the pseudonym of Royal St Marks and was usurped for the film by Stoke Park, just down the road from Pinewood Studios. His opponent, Goldfinger, who plays with a "Dunlop 65 — Number One", may have intoned "Strict Rules of Golf" on the first tee, but the pair would have been invited to the Referee's office in a more formal competition.

Mr Polwinkle, however, once he realises just whose putter he is using, sails on his way, forcing Darwin to make a dangerous admission. "It is a well-known fact that when golf is faultless there is next to nothing to write about it. The golfing reporter may say that So-and-So pushed his drive and pulled his second; but the real fact is that the great So-and-So was on the course with his tee shot, on the green with his second, and down in two putts — and kept on doing it." Remind you of anyone? "That is all the reporter need have said, but he says more because he has his living to earn."

Well, quite. But, however faultless a performance, the story of the latest Great So-and-So — or Champion Golfer of the Year — needs chronicling.

OPEN QUALIFYING SERIES

AUSTRALIA
Emirates Australian Open
-8 December 2019
Matt Jones, Australia
Aaron Pike, Australia
Takumi Kanaya, Japan

AFRICA
South African Open
9-12 January 2020
Branden Grace, South Africa
Marcus Armitage, England
Jaco Ahlers, South Africa

SINGAPORE
SMBC Singapore Open
16-19 January 2020
Richard T Lee, Canada
Poom Saksansin, Thailand
Ryosuke Kinoshita, Japan

USA
Arnold Palmer Invitational
presented by Mastercard
5-8 March 2020
Joel Dahmen, USA
Keith Mitchell, USA

FINAL QUALIFYING

HOLLINWELL
9 June
Daniel Hillier, New Zealand
Richard Mansell, England
Jonathan Thomson, England

PRINCE'S
29 June
Deyen Lawson, Australia
Sam Forgan, England
Connor Worsdall, England

ST ANNES OLD LINKS
29 June
Ben Hutchinson, England
Sam Bairstow [A], England
Gonzalo Fernandez-Castano, Spain

WEST LANCASHIRE
29 June
Nicholas Poppleton, England
Daniel Croft, England

EXEMPT COMPETITORS

Byeong Hun An, Korea	17	**Charley Hoffman**, USA	4	**Carlos Ortiz**, Mexico	4
Abraham Ancer, Mexico	4,13,17	**Max Homa**, USA	4	**Ryan Palmer**, USA	
Daniel Berger, USA	4	**Billy Horschel**, USA	4	**CT Pan**, Chinese Taipei	1
Christiaan Bezuidenhout, South Africa	4,5,6,20	**Sam Horsfield**, England	4	**Victor Perez**, France	4,5,
Richard Bland, England	8	**Rikuya Hoshino**, Japan	22	**Ian Poulter**, England	
Keegan Bradley, USA	4	**Viktor Hovland**, Norway	4	**Jon Rahm**, Spain	4,5,9,13,14
Christoffer Bring [A], Denmark	28	**Mackenzie Hughes**, Canada	4	**Aaron Rai**, England	6
Dean Burmester, South Africa	8	**Yuki Inamori**, Japan	21	**Chez Reavie**, USA	13
Sam Burns, USA	4	**Jazz Janewattananond**, Thailand	18	**Patrick Reed**, USA	3,4,6,10,13,14,1
Rafa Cabrera Bello, Spain	5	**Dustin Johnson**, USA	4,9,10,13,14,17	**JC Ritchie**, South Africa	20
Jorge Campillo, Spain	5	**Rikard Karlberg**, Sweden	33	**Justin Rose**, England	4,13
Patrick Cantlay, USA	4,13,17	**Martin Kaymer**, Germany	4	**Antoine Rozner**, France	4
Paul Casey, England	4,5,13	**Brad Kennedy**, Australia	19	**Xander Schauffele**, USA	4,13,14,1
John Catlin, USA	4	**Chan Kim**, USA	21	**Scottie Scheffler**, USA	4,14
Ricardo Celia, Colombia	16	**Marcus Kinhult**, Sweden	5	**Matthias Schmid** [A], Germany	28
Stewart Cink, USA	1,4	**Chris Kirk**, USA	4	**Marcel Schneider**, Germany	32
Darren Clarke, Northern Ireland	1,2	**Kevin Kisner**, USA	4,13	**Matthias Schwab**, Austria	
Corey Conners, Canada	4,13	**Kurt Kitayama**, USA	5	**Adam Scott**, Australia	4,13,1
Jason Day, Australia	11	**Brooks Koepka**, USA	3,4,9,11,13	**Jason Scrivener**, Australia	8
Bryson DeChambeau, USA	4,9,13,17	**Jason Kokrak**, USA	4,13	**Jack Senior**, England	33
Thomas Detry, Belgium	35	**Matt Kuchar**, USA	13,17	**Laird Shepherd** [A], England	20
Ernie Els, South Africa	1,2	**Romain Langasque**, France	5	**Marcel Siem**, Germany	34
Harris English, USA	4	**Min Woo Lee**, Australia	35	**Webb Simpson**, USA	4,12,13,17
Tony Finau, USA	3,4,13,17	**Marc Leishman**, Australia	4,13,17	**Cameron Smith**, Australia	4,17
Matt Fitzpatrick, England	4,5,6	**Haotong Li**, China	5,17	**Brandt Snedeker**, USA	13
Tommy Fleetwood, England	3,4,5,6,13	**Yuxin Lin** [A], China	30	**Jordan Spieth**, USA	1,2,4
Rickie Fowler, USA	3,13,17	**Adam Long**, USA	4	**Brendan Steele**, USA	
Ryan Fox, New Zealand	19	**Joe Long** [A], England	26	**Henrik Stenson**, Sweden	1,2
Dylan Frittelli, South Africa	4	**Mike Lorenzo-Vera**, France	5	**Kevin Streelman**, USA	
Abel Gallegos [A], Argentina	31	**Shane Lowry**, Republic of Ireland	1,2,3,4,5	**Andy Sullivan**, England	
Sergio Garcia, Spain	4,5,10	**Joost Luiten**, Netherlands	5	**Justin Thomas**, USA	4,11,12,13,14,1
Lucas Glover, USA	13	**Robert MacIntyre**, Scotland	3,4,5	**Brendon Todd**, USA	4
Talor Gooch, USA	4	**Rory McIlroy**, Northern Ireland	1,2,4,5,12,13,14	**Cameron Tringale**, USA	
Lanto Griffin, USA	4	**Troy Merritt**, USA	4	**Erik van Rooyen**, South Africa	5
Emiliano Grillo, Argentina	4	**Phil Mickelson**, USA	1,2,4,11	**Daniel van Tonder**, South Africa	5
Adam Hadwin, Canada	17	**Guido Migliozzi**, Italy	8	**Harold Varner III**, USA	
Cole Hammer [A], USA	29	**Francesco Molinari**, Italy	1,2,5,7	**Johannes Veerman**, USA	33
Justin Harding, South Africa	5	**Collin Morikawa**, USA	4,6,11,14	**Jimmy Walker**, USA	1
Brian Harman, USA	4	**Sebastian Munoz**, Colombia	14	**Matt Wallace**, England	5
Padraig Harrington, Republic of Ireland	1	**Ryutaro Nagano**, Japan	24	**Paul Waring**, England	5
Tyrrell Hatton, England	3,4,5,6,7,14	**Joaquin Niemann**, Chile	4,17	**Lee Westwood**, England	3,4,6
Benjamin Hebert, France	5	**Alex Noren**, Sweden	7	**Bernd Wiesberger**, Austria	5
Russell Henley, USA	4	**Shaun Norris**, South Africa	23	**Danny Willett**, England	3,5,7,10
				Gary Woodland, USA	9,13,1
				Will Zalatoris, USA	4

KEY TO EXEMPTIONS FOR THE 149TH OPEN

Exemptions for 2021 were granted to the following:

(1)   The Open Champions aged 60 or under on 19 July 2020.

(2)   The Open Champions for 2010-2019.

(3)   First 10 and anyone tying for 10th place in The 148th Open at Royal Portrush in 2019.

(4)   The first 50 players on the OWGR for Week 21, 2021, with additional players and reserves drawn from the highest ranked non-exempt players in the weeks prior to The Open.

(5)   First 30 in the Final Race to Dubai Rankings for 2019.

(6)   First 10 in the Final Race to Dubai Rankings for 2020.

(7)   The BMW PGA Championship winners for 2017-2020.

(8)   First five European Tour members and any European Tour members tying for fifth place, not otherwise exempt, in the top 20 of the Race to Dubai Rankings on completion of the 2021 BMW International Open.

(9)   The US Open Champions for 2016-2021.

(10) The Masters Tournament Champions for 2016-2021.

(11) The PGA Champions for 2015-2021.

(12) THE PLAYERS Champions for 2018-2021.

(13) Top 30 players from the Final 2019 FedExCup Points List.

(14) Top 10 players from the Final 2020 FedExCup Points List.

(15) First five PGA TOUR members and any PGA TOUR members tying for fifth place, not exempt in the top 20 of the PGA TOUR FedExCup Points List for 2021 on completion of the 2021 Travelers Championship.

(16) The 114th VISA Open de Argentina 2019 Champion.

(17) Playing members of the 2019 Presidents Cup Teams.

(18) First and anyone tying for first place on the Final Order of Merit of the Asian Tour for 2019.

(19) First and anyone tying for first place on the Final Order of Merit of the PGA Tour of Australasia for 2019 & 2020.

(20) First and anyone tying for first place on the Final Order of Merit of the Sunshine Tour for 2019 & 2020.

(21) The Japan Open Champion for 2019 & 2020.

(22) The Asia-Pacific Diamond Cup Champion for 2020 & 2021.

(23) First two and anyone tying for second place on the Final Official Money List of the Japan Golf Tour for 2019.

(24) First two, not already exempt, in the 2021 Mizuno Open.

(25) The Senior Open Champion for 2019.

(26) The Amateur Champion for 2020 & 2021.

(27) The US Amateur Champion for 2019 & 2020.

(28) The European Amateur Champion for 2020 & 2021.

(29) The Mark H McCormack Medal (Men's World Amateur Golf Ranking®) winner for 2019 & 2020.

(30) The Asia-Pacific Amateur Champion 2019.

(31) The Latin America Amateur Champion 2020.

(32) The leading golfer, not already exempt, who has made the cut, in the 2021 Kaskada Golf Challenge.

(33) First three, not already exempt, who have made the cut, in the 2021 Dubai Duty Free Irish Open.

(34) The leading golfer, not already exempt, who has made the cut, in the 2021 Le Vaudreuil Golf Challenge.

(35) First three, not already exempt, who have made the cut, in the 2021 abrdn Scottish Open.

'On the tee' ... The Open returns

Peter Dixon on the excitement as play resumes at golf's original Championship

Final preparations at dawn for The 149ᵗʰ Open by the greenkeeping staff at Royal St George's led by Paul Larsen (below).

For Paul Larsen, the head greenkeeper at Royal St George's, this had been a second Open Championship in two years.

He had the unique distinction in that he had twice prepared the famed Sandwich links for the oldest and most distinguished of the four major championships.

First in 2020, only to see the Championship cancelled because of Covid-19, and again in 2021. A year earlier, working on the principle of "waste not, want not", the members of Royal St George's got to play it instead and perhaps allowed themselves to dream of holding aloft the Claret Jug on the immaculately prepared 18th green.

In the early hours of Thursday morning, Larsen woke up after what he described as his best sleep in weeks. "It wasn't long, but at least it was deep!" He had been running, he said, on pure adrenaline.

"It's been a journey! Covid, furlough, drought, floods, rain in summer, sweat, tears, hugs — but mostly it's been pure determination, passion, enthusiasm and skill by an amazing team," he revealed on Twitter as the preparations drew to a close.

As dawn broke it was impossible to contradict a master craftsman who, to the delight of anybody who met him, looked more rock musician than man of the turf. What was to greet 156 of the world's finest men's players that day was a course brought to a peak of perfection, in a setting that was second to none. England's version, many would say, of St Andrews, as the club's Scottish founders intended.

As one seasoned observer put it, Royal St George's was looking its absolute best. With its firm, reasonably wide fairways, rough as nature had intended, and firm smooth greens, the course was an exam paper to test all the skills.

On the eve of the Championship, Martin Slumbers, the Chief Executive of The R&A, was delighted: "After such a difficult time in the last year or so for the whole world, I have to admit we are relieved, thrilled and a little bit emotional in being able to stage The Open once again," he said.

Richard Bland, after becoming a first-time winner at the age of 48 in May, had the honour of hitting the first tee shot.

At 6.35am Richard Bland stepped on to the first tee and struck the opening shot. At 48, the Englishman had been given the honour after becoming, in May, the oldest first-time winner of a European Tour event. His British Masters victory at the Belfry came at the 478th attempt and secured him a place in the US Open at Torrey Pines a month later — when he introduced himself to the wider golfing world by sharing the lead after 36 holes — and then The Open on these fabled links on the Kent coast. This was to be only his fifth start in majors spread across four decades.

With just 26 gently spoken words David Lancaster, the official starter, seemed to banish all the angst and disappointment of the previous 12 months.

"Welcome to Royal St George's for the first day's play of The 149th Open," he announced. "This is game number one. On the tee, from England — Richard Bland."

In front of Bland lay a testing opening hole of 445 yards that, in essence, is exactly as it was designed in 1887. The conditions could not have been bettered. There wasn't a cloud in the sky but there was enough of a breeze, expected to come out of the north for most of the week, to keep the flags fluttering atop the 18th green grandstands over his left shoulder.

And accompanying him was Royal St George's very own dawn chorus, the distinctive high-pitched singing of skylarks high above the ground.

Around the first tee, a few hundred spectators — many of whom had bought tickets more than a year earlier — had gathered in the grandstand and along the fairway, keen to witness the first shot of an Open Championship since Shane Lowry sank the winning putt at Royal Portrush two years earlier. They were the advanced guard of the 32,000 spectators who were to come through the gates on each of the four days of play. The sense of excitement was palpable.

And then we were off. With a small nod to the fans, Bland placed his ball on top of his tee, lined up behind it, stepped forward, took a deep breath, and sent the ball on its way. His nerve had held true although as he left the tee he passed Paul McGinley, the former Ryder Cup captain, and called across to him, indicating a shaking hand and saying with a wry smile, "I could have done with a little bit of help to put the ball on the tee peg."

It had been a massive team effort to get The 149th Open up and running. Now it was down to the players to deliver.

And boy, did they deliver.

FIRST ROUND

15 July 2021

A Day When Normal Was Special

By Andy Farrell

It did not take long. No sooner had play got under way for the first time in two years than The Open felt just as it always had.

Richard Bland was followed off the first tee by Andy Sullivan and Marcus Armitage and the 149th edition of the Championship was off and running. Sullivan, whose place in the field was only confirmed the previous weekend, holed a 30-footer on the first green and there was the first birdie.

Everyone had missed this. For good and obvious reasons there was no Open in 2020 and there had been six men's major championships since the raucous scenes when Shane Lowry lifted the Claret Jug at Royal Portrush the year before. There had been Wimbledon and football's European Championship, but now it was golf's turn to light up the British sporting summer.

Even the sun was out, after weeks of rain, a last deluge on Monday stopping the rolling fairways of Royal St George's regaining their fire. But that also meant the rough was up and there was a healthy breeze, unusually for so late in the year, stuck out of the north. "A typical English links day," said Jack Senior, who joined Sullivan on 67, three under par.

And the fans were back, providing a big-time atmosphere. After last year's false start — how differently St George's may have played following that long, sunny, dry spring in 2020 — it had taken countless contingency plans, flexibility to the qualifying process, adaptation to the ever-shifting public health regulations, acceptance by the players and their (smaller than usual) entourages of being restricted solely to the golf course and their accommodation, all the Covid testing and

Louis Oosthuizen led the way on a special day.

vaccinations, a load of pragmatism and no little optimism … but finally 156 players all teed-off and 32,000 spectators were there to watch on each of the Championship days.

"The first tee for me was a special experience," said English debutant Richard Mansell, who made it through Final Qualifying. "You walk out from the tunnel and everyone claps you. It feels like an achievement to be here, which it definitely is, though that's not my mindset.

"It's been a tough 18 months for everyone, us golfers, but also the golf fans," Mansell added. "To have 30,000-odd here every day, it's special. It's something I'm going to remember for the rest of my life. My first major, it definitely didn't disappoint."

Appreciation did not just come from the first-timers, but the regulars as well. "I really love this tournament," said 2017 Champion Golfer Jordan Spieth. "Missing last year was certainly something I didn't want to do.

"Now we're back and inside the ropes it feels the most normal of any tournament that we've played thus far relative to the same tournament in previous years pre-Covid. The fans here are fantastic. They're just the best in golf, very knowledgeable. It was really great to have them back and have what feels like normalcy when we teed-off the first hole."

Spieth radiated enthusiasm for being challenged by links golf once again as the Texan compiled a 65. While compatriot Brian Harman also came in on five under par, another former Champion, Louis Oosthuizen, took the first-round lead with a 64.

It was one better than his previous best at The Open, a 65 with which he opened in 2010 on the way to collecting the Claret Jug. But what he really wanted to

Justin Rose plays his second shot on the 18th hole from near the first tee.

Jon Rahm was the victim of a bunker on the ninth hole on the way to an opening 71.

Birthday boy Siem seizes the day

Given a birthday wish, it's a fair bet that Marcel Siem would have asked for an opening day on the links that would prove to himself and everybody else that he could still hold his own among the game's higher echelons.

The popular German, a four-time winner on the European Tour, lost his card at the end of 2020 and was forced instead to ply his trade on the second-

tier Challenge Tour. It meant he had to play hard just to earn his travel expenses and even carried his own bag before investing in an electric trolley.

Victory in France the week before, his first for seven years, secured a place for Siem in the field at Royal St George's, with the first round coinciding with his 41st birthday.

Could he seize the day? Indeed, he could. With his trademark long hair pulled back into a distinctive bun, he had the look of a player released of all anxiety. There might be work to do, but there was no reason not to enjoy it.

In the event, Siem had an opening round of 67, three under par, to lie just three strokes off the lead and inside the top ten. One over after seven holes, he turned his game around and greeted each of his birdies with a fist-pumping exuberance that delighted the galleries.

"The biggest key for me at the moment is that I'm not getting that upset any more on a golf course," Siem explained. "I'm so grateful to be here."

And everyone was grateful to have him.

After a 67, England's Jack Senior was aiming to make the cut for the first time at his fourth appearance at The Open.

do was go one better than his finishing position at each of the last two majors. After being runner-up at the PGA Championship and the US Open, he had tallied six second places since his only major victory. What was clear was that his form had in no way diminished in moving from Kiawah Island to Torrey Pines to Sandwich.

Teeing-off at 10am alongside the defending Champion Shane Lowry and the US Open winner Jon Rahm, the sweet-swinging South African went serenely about his business as per usual.

"He's very comfortable in himself and that's where you need to be when you're playing in majors," noted two-time Open Champion Padraig Harrington. "He does his thing and doesn't try to be anybody else but Louis. You see that with guys who are playing well. They're happy with who they are."

Pars were Oosthuizen's thing for the first seven holes. "I've learnt over the years in major championships that patience is a key thing," he said. "I was very patient. I didn't hit anything close enough to make birdies on those first few holes, then all of a sudden just made two good putts on eight and nine. That got the ball rolling."

Another 3 at the 10th made it three in a row and then he added two more at the 13th and 14th holes. He had gone from the middle of the pack to sharing the lead in

no time at all. A short putt at the par-3 16th gave him the lead. Six birdies in nine holes, no bogeys across the 18, not even after driving into a bunker at the last. "In my mind, probably the perfect round I could have played," afterwards, said Oosthuizen. "I didn't make many mistakes. When I had opportunities for birdie, I made the putts."

His score was 13 strokes better than his last round on the course, a 77 on the last day in 2011. It also matched the 64 Christy O'Connor Jr returned on the first day in 1985. O'Connor had burst ahead of the field by four that day, while Oosthuizen had just eased himself into a solo lead.

If he made it look easy, the evidence that it was not came from his two playing partners. Both Rahm and Lowry returned 71s. Lowry bogeyed the first two holes from the rough, while Rahm got into bunker trouble at the ninth and had a double-bogey. "Looking at their score afterwards," said Oosthuizen, "I thought they were level or one under, I didn't feel they played poorly.

"If you get out of position off the tee around this course, you're going to find it difficult to give yourself opportunities for birdies. That's the number one, it's hit the fairway. If you aren't comfortable with the driver, then don't be scared laying further back, as long as you can get it in the fairway."

Laying further back was not the plan for a certain

Tommy Fleetwood at the sixth green.

EXCERPTS FROM THE PRESS

"Certainly, these packed galleries made a huge and welcome difference to one man and his doubly vaccinated dog. Since 2019, the country had waited for big-time golf boasting a big-crowd feel and the first day of The 149th Open let nobody down."

—James Corrigan,
The Daily Telegraph

"Oosthuizen displayed the patience of a man who knows that the chase for major glory always is a marathon, but it doesn't hurt to sprint quickly out of the gate."

—Adam Schupak, ***Golfweek***

"The pairing of Jordan Spieth and Bryson DeChambeau feels like a duel for the soul of golf. On the one hand, a traditional figure observing the fundamentals passed down by the ancients. On the other, a golfer rethinking the way the game should be played."

—Kevin Garside, ***iSport***

"The return of spectators made it feel like a proper Open, especially on the hill overlooking the par-3 sixth hole that attracted some of the biggest galleries of the day."

—Steve Douglas,
Associated Press

"Rory McIlroy spent most of the day looking to the heavens in frustration, but his prayers were answered when he birdied the last to open with a level-par 70 that kept his Open hopes alive at Royal St George's."

—Brian Keogh,
Irish Independent

Jordan Spieth searches for the "feel aspect" of links golf during his 65.

A 66 for Webb Simpson, matching his first round at Royal St George's in 2011.

Bryson DeChambeau. Since The Open had last been played, the American had bulked up and won the 2020 US Open but how would "Bryson ball" fare on this old-school links? Initially, not so well. He hit only one fairway in the first 12 holes, four in all, and while there were four birdies, there were also five bogeys in a 71.

DeChambeau was playing with Spieth and Branden Grace, another powerful grouping but one that attracted attention when the tee times were announced because Grace had played the opening rounds with the eventual Champion Golfer of the Year in the last two Opens. "I did hear that," Spieth said. "It just made me laugh. I didn't think much of it." Spieth led DeChambeau by six shots but never for a moment thought it was down to a two-man race.

Spieth made an early bogey but rolled in a long putt from the front of the fifth green and suddenly he was transported back to Royal Birkdale, where he produced a remarkable charge to claim the Claret Jug. The 27-year-old had not won since then until, almost four years later, he won the Valero Texas Open in April. He then finished third at the Masters Tournament and almost won again at the Charles Schwab Challenge in his home state of Texas at Colonial. Not long before he had been stuck in the doldrums. "I've been trending the right way," he said.

That birdie at the fifth was the first of four in a row. He hit his tee shot to six feet at the short sixth, got up and down for a 4 at the seventh and holed from eight feet at the eighth. Animated, engaged, just like old times. He also birdied the 15th and the 16th holes to reach five under par.

Why does links golf bring out the best in Spieth? "It brings the feel aspect into the game," he said. A player battling to regain control of his swing in recent years, he added: "You get less swing-focused and more shot-focused over here because the second you take your brain off what you're hitting, you may not find your ball. There is always a shot you can play to give yourself an advantage, instead of a driving range shot in Palm Springs.

"To sum up, I guess there's a lot of external factors over here, and I think that external is where I need to be living."

Other groups commanded attention on this first day. Harman, the left-hander from Georgia, birdied the first three holes and added another at the fifth and got to five under par at the eighth. "I've been driving well, scrambling and putting well this year, but struggled to get the ball on the green," he said. "But today it was nice to hit some really good iron shots with some command."

Brian Harman was five under par for the first eight holes and finished with a 65.

It's a
FACT

Christy O'Connor Jr set a new course record of 64 in the first round in 1985, subsequently lowered by Nick Faldo and Payne Stewart in 1993. By matching O'Connor's opening effort, Louis Oosthuizen gave himself the chance to better his own record for the lowest opening score by a Champion of 65 from St Andrews in 2010, and equalled by Jordan Spieth in 2017.

EXCERPTS FROM THE PRESS

"Amazing what Danny Willett can do when he's feeling in good health. The man who's had almost as many hospital visits as to the first tee this season opened with a fine 67. Best of all, he wasn't clutching any part of his anatomy as he walked off the 18th green."

—Derek Lawrenson,
Daily Mail

"Jordan Spieth's woes after winning The Open in 2017 were such that he had cause to ponder whether he had fallen victim to some form of Royal and Ancient curse. Spieth looked invincible at Royal Birkdale; by the start of 2021 he sat 92nd in the world. At just 27, he has already encountered golf's extremes."

—Ewan Murray,
The Guardian

"Louis Oosthuizen played like this year's Open was at St Andrews. And Jordan Spieth as if he were back at Royal Birkdale."

—Neil McLeman,
Daily Mirror

"Justin Rose declared 'We're swinging for England' as he led the charge for a first home victory in The Open for 52 years."

—David Facey,
The Sun

"At The Open Arms, there was a festival atmosphere around the big screen. Just across the way was a drop-in NHS vaccination centre, not so much open arms as aching arms."

—John Westerby,
The Times

Canada's Mackenzie Hughes claimed an opening 66.

With son Reagan as his caddie, 2009 Champion Golfer Stewart Cink scored 66.

Harman made two bogeys and two birdies over the rest of the round but there was plenty more action in his group. Mackenzie Hughes made three birdies in a row from the fourth on the way to a 66, which was matched by the third member of the trio, Dylan Frittelli.

"Brian got off to a really hot start and that helped me get into the right mindset," Canadian Hughes said. "It was fun feeding off each other. Walking off 17, I thought, 'Wow, this is quite a group.' We were all four under and Brian birdied the last, so I don't think there will be a group out there that comes close."

There was also a 66 for Stewart Cink, the 2009 Champion Golfer whose form saw a revival with two victories on the 2020-21 PGA Tour season.

Cink did not drop a shot, and nor did France's Benjamin Hebert. He and Webb Simpson, whose 66 matched his very first round in The Open 10 years earlier at St George's, joined those on four under par despite playing late in the afternoon, when the wind got up and the skies turned overcast.

Scoring was over a stroke harder for the later starters and Rory McIlroy, among them, was happy to get in with a 70. More extraordinarily, Phil Mickelson, golf's first 50-something major champion, was 10 strokes worse on 80.

There was a late 67 for Tommy Fleetwood thanks to a birdie at the last as the 2019 runner-up joined a group of English players on three under par. They included Justin Rose, who stayed blemish free on the scorecard despite pulling his drive at the 18th next to a hut by the first tee. Rose played with world number 1 Dustin Johnson, who scored 68, and Will Zalatoris, the Masters Tournament runner-up.

Zalatoris had an adventurous day, holing his second shot at the 12th for an eagle but injuring his back attempting to play from the rough at the 15th. There was also a jabby missed putt of no more than a foot at the 17th in a 69, but the next morning the American was unfit to play and had to withdraw.

Of the 47 rounds under par on Thursday, two-thirds of them came in the morning. Collin Morikawa set off at lunchtime, early in the late wave, and joined the pack at three under par. The rough on the right of the first fairway has never been a good place to hit your first shot at St George's, but the young American, experiencing The Open for the first time, made what

Poppleton puts it all in perspective

They say "never meet your heroes", but for Nick Poppleton the opportunity was too good to miss. The Europro Tour player had come through Regional and Final Qualifying to get to Royal St George's and he wasn't going to pass up the opportunity to mix it with the game's finest.

When the start sheet went up for practice rounds, the 27-year-old Englishman — a supermarket delivery driver and handyman in his spare time — first put his name down alongside Bryson DeChambeau and then discovered that Phil Mickelson would be joining them.

"I saw Bryson's name and I thought, 'Why not?' I'm not shy. But when Phil also put his name down, I was made up. It's a dream come true, isn't it? Playing with these idols." And so it proved, with the two major champions each prepared to offer advice and to share their experiences.

Fair to say that Poppleton arrived on the Kent coast with a healthy dose of perspective. He had seen real pressure at close hand during the pandemic with his girlfriend, Amber, working long, stressful hours as a radiographer at a children's hospital in Sheffield.

Golf suddenly became of secondary importance.

"My role wasn't a golfer," he said, "it became a support for her. That's what it had to be." Hence, the part-time work.

This week, however, was his to savour. Playing in the final group in the first round, Poppleton came in with a respectable 75. It was four more than DeChambeau, but five better than Mickelson. Now that's what memories are made of.

France's Benjamin Hebert did not drop a stroke in a 66, his lowest score in The Open on his third appearance.

Will Zalatoris suffered an injury in the rough during his 69.

An 80 for PGA Champion Phil Mickelson.

he called an "interesting par" via the rough on the other side of the fairway.

He soon settled down and made a 2 at the third hole. In fact, three of his four birdies came at the short holes on a day when he dropped only one shot. "I made some putts and that was important for me," he said. "Huge momentum heading into the next few days."

Of his first look at a traditional links, Morikawa said:

"Being creative is what I do. I love to work the ball, love to figure out different heights you have to hit it, see different windows. That's what links golf tests. I think it fits right into my pocket with that."

Ominous words. But the overriding feeling on Thursday evening was, as Spieth indicated, that having The Open back was at the same time normal, and very, very special.

Round of the Day: Louis Oosthuizen – 64

Six birdies for Oosthuizen and a card kept clean by a 10-foot par save at the last.

> *It's probably the one event of the year where you don't mind getting up early. For other events, you drag yourself out of bed. You've always got a buzz to come and play The Open.*
> —**Andy Sullivan**

> *Hopefully Royal St George's with the St George's cross is kind of a lucky omen this week.*
> —**Justin Rose**

> *It was wonderful to be back. The reception I got on the first tee and the first fairway was great.*
> —**Darren Clarke**

> *There's 13 of us from South Africa playing this week. We've got a strong contingent and they're all capable of playing well.*
> —**Justin Harding**

> *There's a lot of crosswind. This is a course which is sort of turning, so you rarely get the same wind twice. We only played two or three holes downwind today.*
> —**Paul Casey**

> *I had loads of people in the crowd that I knew. And the birdie on three, when I rolled that in it was like I won the tournament there was so many people shouting out.*
> —**Sam Forgan**

> *I think for my first major, I was enjoying it until I made my triple-bogey.*
> —**Min Woo Lee**

> *It was quite brutal out there this afternoon, windy, gusty. I don't think the morning boys quite had the gust.*
> —**Cameron Smith**

After an "interesting par" at the opening hole, Collin Morikawa settled down and began his first Open with a 67.

A traditional scoreboard in the tented village, where spectators could also follow Thursday's early action online.

FIRST ROUND LEADERS

HOLE	1	2	3	4	5	6	7	8	9	OUT	10	11	12	13	14	15	16	17	18	IN	TOTAL
PAR	4	4	3	4	4	3	5	4	4	35	4	3	4	4	5	4	3	4	4	35	70
Louis Oosthuizen	4	4	3	4	4	3	5	3	3	33	3	3	4	3	4	4	2	4	4	31	64
Jordan Spieth	4	4	4	4	3	2	5	3	4	32	4	3	4	4	5	3	2	4	4	33	65
Brian Harman	3	3	2	4	3	3	5	3	5	31	4	3	5	3	5	4	3	4	3	34	65
Mackenzie Hughes	4	4	3	3	3	2	5	4	4	32	3	3	3	4	5	5	3	4	4	34	66
Dylan Frittelli	4	4	3	4	4	4	4	3	4	34	4	2	4	4	4	4	3	3	4	32	66
Stewart Cink	4	4	3	4	4	2	5	4	4	34	3	3	4	3	4	4	3	4	4	32	66
Benjamin Hebert	4	4	2	3	4	3	5	4	4	33	3	3	4	4	4	4	3	4	4	33	66
Webb Simpson	4	4	2	4	4	3	6	4	4	34	3	3	4	3	4	4	2	4	4	32	66
Andy Sullivan	3	4	3	4	3	6	3	3	5	34	3	4	4	4	5	3	3	4	3	33	67
Justin Harding	4	4	3	4	4	2	7	3	4	35	4	3	4	4	4	2	3	4		32	67
Danny Willett	3	4	3	4	3	4	6	4	4	35	3	4	4	3	4	4	3	4	4	32	67
Jack Senior	3	4	3	4	4	3	5	3	4	33	4	3	4	3	5	4	3	4	4	34	67
Justin Rose	3	4	3	4	4	4	5	3	4	34	3	3	4	3	5	4	3	4	4	33	67
Scottie Scheffler	4	4	2	4	4	3	4	4	4	33	5	4	4	3	4	4	3	3	4	34	67
Byeong Hun An	3	4	3	4	4	3	5	4	4	32	4	3	4	5	5	4	3	3	4	35	67
Collin Morikawa	4	4	2	4	5	2	5	3	4	33	4	4	4	4	5	4	2	4	4	34	67
Marcel Siem	4	4	3	4	4	3	6	3	3	34	3	3	4	3	5	4	2	4	4	33	67
Tommy Fleetwood	4	4	3	5	4	2	5	4	3	34	3	3	3	4	5	4	3	4	3	33	67

■ EAGLE OR BETTER   ■ BIRDIES   ☐ PAR   ■ OVER PAR

SCORING SUMMARY

FIRST ROUND SCORES

Players Under Par	47
Players At Par	26
Players Over Par	83

LOW SCORES

Low First Nine
Brian Harman — 31

Low Second Nine
Louis Oosthuizen — 31

Low Round
Louis Oosthuizen — 64

FIRST ROUND HOLE SUMMARY

HOLE	PAR	YARDS	EAGLES	BIRDIES	PARS	BOGEYS	D.BOGEYS	OTHER	RANK	AVERAGE
1	4	441	0	33	83	36	4	0	11	4.071
2	4	410	0	10	115	28	3	0	5	4.154
3	3	217	0	17	113	23	3	0	10	3.077
4	4	497	0	22	102	28	4	0	9	4.090
5	4	408	0	11	105	36	3	1	3	4.218
6	3	175	0	47	98	11	0	0	17	2.769
7	5	547	0	22	96	33	5	0	7	5.135
8	4	444	0	31	105	20	0	0	15	3.929
9	4	408	0	9	105	38	3	1	2	4.244
OUT	35	3,547	0	202	922	253	25	2		35.686
10	4	417	0	20	112	22	2	0	12	4.038
11	3	214	0	7	113	34	2	0	4	3.199
12	4	366	2	29	100	23	2	0	14	3.962
13	4	448	0	21	92	42	0	1	5	4.154
14	5	551	1	80	63	9	2	1	18	4.577
15	4	490	0	7	89	57	2	1	1	4.365
16	3	156	0	42	103	11	0	0	16	2.801
17	4	416	1	17	114	23	1	0	12	4.038
18	4	444	0	15	111	24	6	0	7	4.135
IN	35	3,502	4	238	897	245	17	3		35.269
TOTAL	70	7,049	4	440	1,819	498	42	5		70.955

Fun for Jordan but rough for Bryson

Alistair Tait watches a contrast in styles play out over the links

Links golf doesn't always reward brute strength. Sometimes finesse matters much more.

That juxtaposition was in evidence in the respective approaches of Jordan Spieth and Bryson DeChambeau as they played alongside each other in the opening round of The 149th Open at Royal St George's.

Spieth had developed an admiration and understanding for the Sandwich links by the time he arrived on the first tee on Thursday morning. It was perhaps not surprising he returned a 65, five under par, to finish the day tied for second place with fellow American Brian Harman, one shot behind South African Louis Oosthuizen.

DeChambeau? He hit just four fairways in his 71, one over par, proof that the hit-it-as-far-as-you-can tactic he used to win the 2020 US Open at Winged Foot isn't a recipe for success over Royal St George's, arguably the most quintessential of the Open Championship links.

Yet that was DeChambeau's game plan: batter St George's into submission and walk off with the Claret Jug.

"I hope I can hit it far enough to where I can wedge it out still onto the green if I get good enough lies," DeChambeau said in his pre-Championship press conference. "I hope that the length will be a little bit of an advantage. I just have to drive it well."

DeChambeau praised Tiger Woods's approach in winning The Open in 2006 when he sat down with the world's media ahead of the Championship. Woods hit 2-iron around Royal Liverpool to keep the ball in play, and walked off with his third Claret Jug.

"He showcased an awesome ability to play it on the ground, play links on the ground, which is the way it should be played I personally think ... albeit I do something completely different," the Californian said.

Different didn't work out well for DeChambeau in round one. You didn't have to look hard to find images of the 27-year-old in knee-high rough, clumps of grass hanging off the hosel of his clubs as he tried to gouge his ball out of the deep grass off the St George's fairways.

The hit-it-long-and-far approach backfired on the opening hole. DeChambeau found the rough off the tee en route to an opening bogey. His four fairways hit

Jordan Spieth, the 2017 Champion Golfer, felt good about his chances after an opening 65 on this "fun, cool track".

Bryson DeChambeau spent much of the day in the rough as his attempt to overpower the links with power led to a 71.

stat led him to make a blunt complaint about the longest club in his bag. "The driver sucks," he said. His comment drew sharp rebuke from equipment manufacturer Cobra. DeChambeau, perhaps remembering the old adage about a good craftsman never blaming his tools, had the good grace to issue a public apology.

Spieth had no cause to complain about his equipment. He put on a masterclass in shaping shots around The Open's most southerly links, showing the same nous that helped him become the 2017 Champion Golfer of the Year at Royal Birkdale. But then the Texan had already fallen in love with St George's after just 12 holes of his first practice round.

"I've come into venues I've never seen before in any tournament, not just an Open, and I've always just tried to find something I love about it," the 27-year-old American said.

"There have been times recently where I've said, 'Man, I just really don't like this place'. I came in here and I've been in a really good mood about it. My first walk around it I played 12 holes, played a loop on Sunday, and it was the opposite wind and I thought, 'Man, this could be a really fun, kind of cool, tricky track'."

The three-time major champion even went as far as to compare St George's to Royal Birkdale, despite links afficionados quick to point out the latter course's flatter fairways.

"Birkdale was a course that you played a lot from the air versus other Open venues," Spieth explained. "You couldn't really bounce it up a ton there, and you really can't bounce it up a ton here. So, it has similarities on that front, where it's more of an aerial links. You've got to flight the ball but you can't really get away with kind of punching five clubs extra up the entire green. You can on some holes, but there's bunkers that guard the fronts and there's a lot of false fronts here."

Spieth certainly flighted his ball well in his opening round. No wonder he was in a good mood after his first competitive round on the links Dr Laidlaw Purves originally laid out in 1887.

"I feel really good about my chances going forward, as good as they have been historically."

He had every right to feel positive: his 65 matched his lowest first-round score in The Open, which he posted at Royal Birkdale.

DeChambeau's 71 put him among the chasing peloton in a tie for 74th. He walked off St George's perhaps wondering if maybe Woods's 2006 approach was worth a try after all. By Sunday, he knew it was.

SECOND ROUND

16 July 2021

Records Galore at Sandwich

By Andy Farrell

If Thursday's golf was good, Friday's was even better. It was record-breaking.

"I'm awful with golf history," said Collin Morikawa, and that was all right because it was being rewritten right in front of us.

"I just want to create my own memories," added the 24-year-old Californian. He certainly did that with a round of 64 but had no idea that he had finished one shy of equalling the course record of 63. So no place in the history books yet — that would have to wait for Sunday.

Instead, the second round of The 149th Open saw plenty of other records tumble at Royal St George's:

Louis Oosthuizen, whose one-stroke overnight lead had become a three-shot deficit by the time he teed off on Friday afternoon, added a 65 to his own 64 to complete 36 holes with a total of 129 — one better than the record set by Sir Nick Faldo at Muirfield in 1992 and equalled by Brandt Snedeker at Royal Lytham & St Annes in 2012.

The halfway cut fell on a total of 141, two strokes lower than the previous record of 143 set nine times between 1990 and 2019. Those included the Championships at Sandwich in 1993 and 2011.

There were 63 rounds under the par of 70 on Friday, not just a higher number than Thursday's 47, but shattering the previous record for a single round of 50 from the first day at Turnberry in 2009.

Among those rounds under par was a 65 by Matthias Schmid, which matched the lowest round by an amateur at The Open set by England's Tom Lewis at St George's in the first round in 2011. Schmid, a 23-year-old from Germany, was the 2019 and 2020

Collin Morikawa making his own memories with a 64.

European Amateur champion. He had opened with a 74 on Thursday but did not drop a stroke on Friday and birdied four of the last seven holes to comfortably ensure making the cut.

His 65, from the third game of what at that stage was a chilly morning, put Schmid in glittering company as Oosthuizen, defending Champion Shane Lowry, world number 1 Dustin Johnson and Harris English also achieved that score.

But it was not the lowest of the day as Morikawa was joined on 64 by Emiliano Grillo and Jon Rahm. Grillo, finishing just after the American, saw his approach shot at the 18th spin across the hole. He tapped in for his ninth birdie of the day, six of them coming on the second nine.

"I'll take 64 for any round in a major," said the 28-year-old from Argentina, who beat his best score in his four previous Opens by four strokes.

"The people made it so nice out there. It almost felt like I was playing with my buddies back home. Blue skies with not much wind, it's definitely a day where you're going to see a lot of good scores."

Grillo matched the clubhouse total of six under par set by Daniel van Tonder with an early 66. It was the mark on which Oosthuizen led overnight but actually held up well on the leaderboard for most of the day until a flood of good scores in the evening. Andy Sullivan also reached that total with a second 67 to be the leading English contender, as did Marcel Siem, who might have set a record for the number of fist pumps for the Championship but, sadly, official verification was unavailable. Siem also lost his distinction of having the lowest score by a 41-year-old on their birthday, as Adam Scott returned a 66.

By now Morikawa was on top by three strokes.

EXCERPTS FROM THE PRESS

"Dust down the King Louis headlines and prepare a fresh page in the record books. Golf's most elegant machine purred for 18 holes as Oosthuizen smashed a halfway scoring record set by Sir Nick Faldo that had stood since 1992."

—Derek Lawrenson,
Daily Mail

"While Oosthuizen holds pole position, he has some serious rivals tucked in behind. Unexpectedly benign conditions kept scoring low, but the quality of the competition can hardly be doubted when the top-three places are occupied by men who already have major titles to their names."

—Alasdair Reid,
The Times

"Morikawa got it started Friday morning with a round so pure that it looked as though he might have a chance to set the major championship record at 61."

—Doug Ferguson,
Associated Press

"Shane Lowry is still the king of the jungle in The Open, and he's vowed to go big-game hunting as the game's predators closed in on the leaders. The reigning Champion was determined not to let his long-awaited title defence peter out with a whimper, and he made sure he roared loudly on a traditional ice-cream cone Open afternoon in Sandwich."

—Brian Keogh,
Irish Independent

Daniel van Tonder scored 66 assisted by his wife, and caddie, Abigail.

Shane Lowry had a 65 playing alongside Oosthuizen (65) and Rahm (64).

Louis Oosthuizen hits his tee shot at the 16th hole on the day he broke The Open record for the lowest 36-hole total.

That is how far ahead he was of anyone on his half of the draw, the late-early side, which due to the weather on the first two days proved almost two and a half shots harder than for the early-lates. It was a peerless exhibition of ball-striking, enabled by switching his irons after finishing 71st at the abrdn Scottish Open the previous week.

That was Morikawa's first experience of playing on fescue surfaces and he found the ball sitting slightly differently than usual. "I couldn't find the centre of the clubface," he admitted. Once he made the change, he couldn't miss it. "Last week I wanted to win, but I came out of it learning a lot more." Yet while The Renaissance Club is a modern, links-like layout, Royal St George's is the 134-year-old real McCoy. For his first crack at The Open, however, Morikawa did just as he had in his two years on tour, "figuring out on the golf course Monday through Wednesday what I need to do to play well.

"Yeah, Royal St George's is beautiful," he added. "I think it fits into a lot of shots that I love to hit. When I'm in the middle of the fairway with a 9-iron, an 8-iron, or a 7-iron, I feel very comfortable. Not necessarily going straight at the pins, but being aggressive with the lines I need to take and the slopes you need to play."

"That's my bread and butter. That's what I love to do. When I'm in the middle of the fairway, I feel I can hit it just as close as some guys with their wedges, especially when I'm on like the first two days.

"Today I hit a few more fairways, a few more early in the round, and sometimes you have days where you're very fortunate to have good numbers. Today was one of those days."

It certainly was. Where he had tangled with the rough on the first hole on Thursday, this morning he only needed a wedge for his approach and put it to five feet for an opening birdie. At the fifth, he was even closer and though the putter did the business from 25 feet at the eighth, at the next hole he hit his 8-iron to two feet. Four birdies and he was out in 31 strokes. No one bettered that all day.

Morikawa was also now leading at seven under par having edged past Oosthuizen. At the 11th he sent a 5-iron to 12 feet from the hole for a 2, then wedged to three feet at the 12th. He drove into a bunker at the 13th, was forced to splash out but saved his par with a pitch and a putt.

"That saved the day," he said.

At least, it meant no loss of momentum heading to the par-5 14th, where he secured a 4. He was 10 under par and leading by four.

The par-5 seventh hole.

"It was impressive to watch," said playing partner Corey Conners. "Collin played amazing golf."

Morikawa's only slip up came at the next, after finding the rough off the tee and finishing just short of the green in two. So he needed one more birdie to match the course record held by Faldo and Payne Stewart from 1993. "I had no clue what any course record was," Morikawa said. His putt for a birdie at the last from eight feet touched the edge of the hole but stayed out.

Morikawa's clubhouse lead at nine under par was not threatened until Jordan Spieth and Oosthuizen teed off in the afternoon. Spieth birdied the first two holes and although he got to nine under par at one point, while others were making hay over the closing stretch, he played the last six holes in one over par. "That was frustrating," he said. "I didn't stay focused. I got into a weird headspace, like fatigued, on the 13th green." He was planning to bring more food with him for Saturday's round.

Spieth finished the day at eight under par and in third place. Oosthuizen merely picked up where he left off on Thursday. A birdie at the first. Another at the par-5 seventh. It was a run of four under par for three holes on the back nine that catapulted the 2010 Champion Golfer past Morikawa. He hit a wedge to a foot at the 12th, an 8-iron to 10 feet at the next and, at the 14th, gloriously ran a 4-iron up onto the green and holed from 20 feet for the eagle. Suddenly, the South African was leading by three strokes.

His attempt to become the first player to complete the first two rounds without dropping a shot since Brandt Snedeker in 2012 stalled at the 16th, where he found the bunker on the right of the green where Thomas Bjorn took three to escape in 2003. Oosthuizen exited the trap first time but missed the putt for par. The green was probably still rocking from Jonathan Thomson having caused the biggest roar of the day by holing in one.

Oosthuizen holed a good putt on 17 not to drop two shots in a row and signed for his 65 and that new record tally of 129. "I wasn't aware of that, but to have any record at The Open is always very special," Oosthuizen said. He led by two strokes from Morikawa and three from Spieth. "My game is good, but I know it's a really good leaderboard," he added.

"I have to play good golf this weekend if I want to come out first. Around this golf course, a lot of things can happen. I remember at St Andrews in 2010, I know I had a big lead, but the first time I thought about winning was after the tee shot at 17 on Sunday."

It had turned into a delightful summer's evening, the sun still shining and the breeze dropping away. "I would say we got lucky the last nine holes," Oosthuizen said. "All of us took advantage." His was the premier group of the day. Lowry also had a 65 and

It's a FACT

Before this year, the record halfway cut at The Open of 143 occurred nine times at seven different courses from 1990 to 2019, including twice at Royal St George's in 1993 and 2011. In 2021 at the same venue, 77 players qualified for the weekend with a total no worse than 141, one over par.

Jordan Spieth remained in contention with a 67 to be eight under.

Nine birdies for Argentina's Emiliano Grillo in one of three 64s on Friday as he finished at six under par.

Shepherd attempts another rally

Could the comeback king do it again?

Laird Shepherd never stopped battling to win the Amateur Championship at Nairn in June. He scored seven shots better in the second strokeplay round to qualify on the mark, then scrapped his way through to the final where he was eight down after 17 holes to Monty Scowsill. Shepherd was still seven down with 14 to play and needed to win the last four holes to force a play-off. The 23-year-old University of Stirling graduate capped a remarkable rally by eventually winning at the 38th.

His reward was a place in The Open at Royal St George's, just along the coast from Rye Golf Club, where the Brighton-born Shepherd is a member. So there were plenty of family and friends watching him play at Sandwich, including his girlfriend, Chloe Goadby, the 2021 Scottish Women's Amateur champion.

After an opening 74, Shepherd dropped three shots on the first two holes on Friday before he set about another comeback. There were 2s at both the third and the sixth, the latter sparking a run of five birdies in eight holes. He finished two strokes shy of qualifying for the weekend but posted a 69 in the company of Danny Willett and Dean Burmester.

"The whole experience has been amazing," said Shepherd. "It's great that the people closest to me could be here and I'm happy to play relatively decent over the last few holes to entertain them. The biggest thing has been to learn from the guys. Danny and Dean played great and it's been good to see where my game needs to improve."

Jon Rahm's second at the last hole.

Scottie Scheffler, the 2020 PGA Tour Rookie of the Year, continued to enjoy his debut in The Open with a 66.

US Open champion Rahm got his Championship into gear with the third 64 of the day. The Spaniard was the third player of the day to come close to tying the course record, his putt at the last pulling up a roll short.

There was a 66 for Brooks Koepka, despite an early double-bogey, to get to five under par, while suddenly there was a trio on seven under with Johnson scoring another 65, Scottie Scheffler a 66 and Dylan Frittelli a 67. When Harris English posted his 65, it was the 11th score of 65 or better over the two days. In 14 previous Opens at Sandwich, there had only ever been a total of 10.

It was not the best day for the English themselves, but English the American matched Grillo in coming home in 30 strokes. Standing on the ninth tee, he was six over par. "I don't like missing the cut, and I especially don't like missing the cut at The Open," English said. He finished at level par, one inside the record low cut, qualifying for the fifth time in his sixth Open. Among those making the cut on the mark at one over par were Bryson DeChambeau, Robert MacIntyre, after making a 10-footer at the last, Rickie Fowler, English qualifier Richard Mansell and left-handed Chinese amateur Yuxin Lin, who would provide Schmid with competition for the Silver Medal over the weekend.

Ian Poulter went out in four-under-par 31 during his 66.

A second 67 for Andy Sullivan, the leading Englishman after two days.

Germany's Matthias Schmid equalled The Open's amateur record of 65.

"The fiercely patriotic crowds in Sandwich are quite happy to swap allegiances. Tommy Fleetwood started with a gallery up to nine deep on his opening holes. However, after bogeying the eighth and ninth holes, there were quite a few fans thinking out loud: 'Let's go and watch Andy Sullivan, think that might be more fun'."

—Kate Rowan,
The Daily Telegraph

"Jonathan Thomson says his hole-in-one lifted him out of the doldrums. The 6ft 9in world number 889 received the biggest cheer of the day at St George's for his ace on the par-3 16th hole."

—Andrew Dillon,
The Sun

"Daniel van Tonder has revealed the secret of his successful relationship with his wife and caddie Abigail — it is his fault if it goes wrong."

—Neil McLeman,
Daily Mirror

"Emiliano Grillo is savouring the moment. The Argentinian is currently having a ball at The Open. He has also had the pleasure of watching his country lift an inter-national football trophy this past week, something his hosts can't quite say themselves."

—Paul MacInnes,
The Guardian

Jigger stands tall

When Jonathan "Jigger" Thomson stepped on to the tee at the par-3 16th in the second round he was on the cutline and perhaps fearing a weekend at home.

The packed grandstand may have been staring in awe at their first sighting of the tallest player ever to grace the Championship — at 6ft 9in the 25-year-old Englishman towered above all and sundry — but soon he was giving them something else to remember, a majestic hole-in-one with a gap wedge from 149 yards that effectively sealed his place for the final 36 holes.

Nick Dougherty, commentating for Sky Sports, could not contain his delight as the ball cleared a greenside bunker, hopped, skipped, rolled and then disappeared into the bottom of the hole. "He's a mountain of a man and that's his Everest," exclaimed the former European Tour player amid the roars and celebrations.

In truth Jigger — a nickname given to him by his parents for his love of dancing around in nappies as a toddler — had already conquered his Everest. That came at the age of 12 when he was given the all-clear after a five-year battle with leukaemia.

A qualifier at Sandwich, Thomson could barely believe he had achieved an ace in his first Open. "It is just phenomenal to be honest," he said. "The roar, the shot, everything about that hole is indescribable really.

"You dream about playing in The Open as a kid and then you come here, have a hole-in-one and make the cut and it is just like, 'Wow!'"

An Everest moment for man-mountain Jonathan Thomson.

Among those to miss out were the record oldest major winner Phil Mickelson, inevitably after his opening 80, fellow former Champions Stewart Cink, Henrik Stenson and Francesco Molinari, plus Patrick Reed and England's highest ranked player Tyrrell Hatton, after rounds of 72 and 70.

It had been a breathless end to the day, the Championship perfectly poised, but earlier there had been a moment of poignancy on the first tee. In memory of the late Peter Alliss, whose connection with The Open went back 70 years, 60 of them spent adding unforgettable words to the television pictures as the "Voice of Golf", official starter David Lancaster invited the gallery, including Peter's widow Jackie, to pay tribute with a minute's applause.

It was moving and uplifting in equal measure. A moment of reflection amid all the records.

A minute's applause on the first tee celebrated the life of Peter Alliss — watched by his widow Jackie and family.

Darren Clarke, the Champion Golfer of the Year at Sandwich in 2011, was moved by the ovation he received on the 18th green.

Dustin Johnson's second shot at the third hole.

Round of the Day: **Collin Morikawa**

Morikawa studies his putt on the final green that would have tied the course record.

HOLE	1	2	3	4	5	6	7	8	9	OUT	10	11	12	13	14	15	16	17	18	IN	TOTAL
PAR	4	4	3	4	4	3	5	4	4	35	4	3	4	4	5	4	3	4	4	35	70-140
Louis Oosthuizen	3	4	3	4	4	3	4	4	4	33	4	3	3	3	3	4	4	4	4	32	65-129
Collin Morikawa	3	4	3	4	3	3	5	3	3	31	4	2	3	4	4	5	3	4	4	33	64-131
Jordan Spieth	3	3	4	3	4	3	5	4	4	33	3	3	3	4	5	5	3	4	4	34	67-132
Dylan Frittelli	5	4	3	4	4	3	5	4	4	36	4	4	4	4	4	2	3	3	4	31	67-133
Dustin Johnson	4	4	4	3	4	3	4	4	3	33	4	3	3	4	5	4	5	3	3	32	65-133
Scottie Scheffler	4	5	3	4	4	3	5	3	4	34	4	3	3	4	5	4	3	4	3	32	66-133
Daniel van Tonder	4	4	3	4	5	3	5	3	4	35	4	3	3	4	4	4	3	3	3	31	66-134
Emiliano Grillo	4	3	3	5	3	2	6	4	4	34	3	3	4	3	3	4	3	3	3	30	64-134
Marcel Siem	4	4	4	4	4	3	5	3	4	35	3	3	4	4	4	4	3	3	4	32	67-134
Andy Sullivan	4	4	3	4	3	3	5	4	4	34	4	3	3	4	5	2	4	4	4	33	67-134
Justin Harding	4	4	3	3	5	3	6	4	3	35	3	3	4	4	3	4	3	4	4	32	67-134

■ EAGLE OR BETTER   ■ BIRDIES   □ PAR   ■ OVER PAR

SCORING SUMMARY

SECOND ROUND SCORES

Players Under Par	63
Players At Par	20
Players Over Par	72

LOW SCORES

Low First Nine

Tony Finau	31
Collin Morikawa	31
Ian Poulter	31

Low Second Nine

Emiliano Grillo	30
Harris English	30

Low Round

Collin Morikawa	64
Emiliano Grillo	64
Jon Rahm	64

SECOND ROUND HOLE SUMMARY

HOLE	PAR	YARDS	EAGLES	BIRDIES	PARS	BOGEYS	D.BOGEYS	OTHER	RANK	AVERAGE
1	4	437	0	14	106	27	8	0	5	4.187
2	4	407	0	10	102	39	2	2	3	4.252
3	3	238	0	11	100	43	1	0	4	3.219
4	4	489	0	15	102	32	6	0	5	4.187
5	4	429	0	8	100	40	7	0	2	4.297
6	3	165	0	23	117	13	0	2	10	2.987
7	5	569	4	42	88	18	3	0	16	4.832
8	4	453	0	28	109	18	0	0	11	3.935
9	4	408	0	47	88	18	1	1	15	3.852
OUT	35	3,595	4	198	912	248	28	5		35.748
10	4	411	0	30	92	30	1	2	9	4.052
11	3	184	0	12	115	26	2	0	7	3.116
12	4	365	0	44	95	16	0	0	17	3.819
13	4	455	0	21	95	39	0	0	7	4.116
14	5	542	6	82	51	8	7	1	18	4.555
15	4	497	0	12	81	56	6	0	1	4.361
16	3	149	1	24	124	6	0	0	13	2.871
17	4	423	0	38	101	16	0	0	14	3.858
18	4	454	0	37	98	20	0	0	12	3.890
IN	35	3,480	7	300	852	217	16	3		34.639

t was quite a show. Jon Rahm, Louis Oosthuizen and Shane Lowry were playing together over the first two rounds and, in what was a well-nigh perfect exhibition of golf on the Friday, Rahm returned a 64 to his companions' 65s. There was no wind to influence proceedings; just three great players sweeping each other along in the afternoon sun.

The previous week, at the abrdn Scottish Open, Rahm had talked of how much he relished the unique demands of links golf. "You have a little bit more variety, and then there's the ever-changing weather and the state of the golf course. All those things, along with the element of luck dependant on what part of the draw you're in."

So much had contributed to the Spaniard's mood of the moment in the build-up to what was his first visit to Royal St George's since the Boys' Amateur Championship in 2009, the one where England's Tom Lewis came out on top.

First, his wife, Kelley, had given birth to a baby boy on the weekend before the Masters Tournament. Rahm felt that that, in itself, provided "a bit of a shift in my golf course mentality. I believe it's because I set out to be an example for my son that he would be

proud of. I've done some stuff in the past that I'm not proud of and I wish I could eliminate it.

"Mind you, I'm not saying it's going to be smooth sailing to the end ..."

His physical game was good in building a six-shot lead after 54 holes of the Memorial Tournament, and his mental game even better when he accepted that he had to withdraw with a round to go after testing positive for Covid-19. He told his wife that something good would come out of that wretched situation and it surely did at the US Open as he made those decisive putts on the last two holes at Torrey Pines for his first major title.

At The Open, meantime, he seemed buoyed by a line of questioning which gave him an opportunity to put a stop to the oft-voiced theory that his short swing is down to his hips. "I'm tired," he said, "of hearing that I have tight hips or other things ... If you know anything about golf, it's the stupidest thing to say."

It turned out that he had been born with a club foot on his right leg. The foot was 90 degrees turned inside out and practically upside down. "So when I was born, they basically relocated pretty much every bone in the ankle and I was put in a cast from the knee down, all within the space of 20 minutes," he explained.

Rahm went on to explain that his right ankle did not have the mobility or stability to allow for a longer action: "So I learned at a very early age that I'm going to have to be more efficient at creating power and consistency by using a shorter swing." His wrists, too, are short on mobility, and therefore need to be bowed in a manner which is some way removed from the conventional.

There is no question that Rahm's fans, as they watched him over the first couple of days, would have been discussing the advice which he had delivered towards the end of that story about his early problems: "The biggest lesson I can give any young player," he added, "is don't try to copy me; don't try to copy any swing out there. Just swing your swing. Learn from your body. Your body is going to tell you what it can and can't do'."

His Friday 64 began with what might sound like a straightforward run of five pars when, in fact, the par at the fifth involved a heartening putt which lifted his spirits for birdies at the sixth and seventh. "They gave me the confidence I needed to play really good golf over the last 14 holes," he said.

Following another birdie at the ninth, there were three more from the 13th, with the one at the 15th involving a well-judged wedge and little more than a tap-in.

When it came to the 18th, everyone in the surrounding amphitheatre seemed to be aware that his 15-footer offered the chance of a 63. Alas the rising excitement stalled as the ball stopped one tantalising roll from the hole.

"Tomorrow," he said of how he was six shots behind Oosthuizen, "is the most important day right now. If I can add another solid round like I did today, and the leaders don't go too low, I think that could work. I have the confidence that I can go low on the weekend to win the tournament.

"I'm hoping I don't have to do anything extravagant, but if it needs to be done, I'll try, and I'll have the confidence I can do it."

Jon Rahm just missed out on equalling the course record as the US Open winner got back into contention on Friday.

Louis Looks to Go One Better

By Andy Farrell

Like all good Saturday night dramas, this third round came to a conclusion on a tantalising twist.

There were not the fireworks of Friday evening, but with 54 holes completed, The 149th Open was intriguingly poised. In some ways, little had changed. Louis Oosthuizen still led, for the third day running. Collin Morikawa remained in second place, and Jordan Spieth in third.

Yet, over the four hours or so that the leaders were on the course, plenty had shifted among the sand dunes of Sandwich. No one escapes an Open Championship round at Royal St George's without being changed. The plot had suddenly got a lot richer, even if that was not reflected on the leaderboard.

Although he never lost the lead, for significant parts of the third round Oosthuizen was tied with Spieth. It was developing into a duel between the two former Champion Golfers of the Year for this year's prize. But then came the final three holes.

Oosthuizen, overcoming his most serious wobble of the week to date, birdied the 16th hole to go back in front on his own. Then Spieth bogeyed the last two holes. If taking three to hole out from the bank short of the 17th green was merely careless, missing from no more than two feet on the final green was unforgivable. At least, that was what the American appeared to think about it as he headed straight for the putting green. For more than an hour he worked on grooving his action and cooling his mind.

That left Oosthuizen again at the head of affairs on his own. This was the 10th major championship round in a row where the South African had finished in the top three. Putting himself in position again only

Louis Oosthuizen acknowledges the crowd on the 18th green.

meant having to face more questions about finishing second again — six times since he won The Open in 2010, including at each of the previous two majors.

"Go one better," Oosthuizen said of his intention for the following day. "You know, finishing second isn't great, so I will play my heart out tomorrow and see if I can lift the Claret Jug again.

"I'll do the same thing," he added of his plans for the following morning. "I don't really change my routine whether I've got a one-shot lead or I'm trailing by eight. The only thing that changes is the tee-time.

"I would say you have to keep yourself busy and not let your mind wander. I think all of us are human to think of lifting the trophy, and that's going to be on your mind. But you need to know how to handle it. Once we get to the golf course, it's all golf.

"You need to believe that you can lift the trophy, as well. If you think beforehand that you might win this Championship, I think that is great. You have to believe you can do it."

Building belief was what the third round was all about. Oosthuizen and Spieth both scored 69 but Morikawa had a 68 to cut the lead to one. The young American, after a nervy start to the round, appeared to finish the day stronger given the conditions.

Although the sun shone even brighter, there was still enough breeze to test the competitors, and more of the holes were tucked in less accessible spots. There was not the same amount of low scoring as the previous days. Of those that finished in the top 11 places at the end of the round, on six under par or better, 10 had scores between 68-70, with Corey Conners managing a 66.

Only Robert MacIntyre with an early 65 scored lower on the day. The Scot leapt up from the cutline

Dustin Johnson, a runner-up in 2011, was uncharacteristically out of sorts with five bogeys in the first 11 holes.

Corey Conners lining up a putt on the 10th hole, the first of four birdies in five holes as he came home in 31.

helped by birdies at the last two holes. Rory McIlroy also looked to be making a charge when he went out in 31, but the Northern Irishman stalled coming home for a 69. Of the English, Paul Casey and Andy Sullivan finished best placed, but at five under par, they were seven strokes adrift. Shane Lowry, the defending Champion, was on the same mark.

Among the surprises of this third round was Dustin Johnson, the runner-up at St George's in 2011, starting out with five bogeys in the first 11 holes and the first of two birdies not arriving until the 14th. He had a 73, while Brooks Koepka bogeyed three of the first five holes in a 72. Jon Rahm, after his 64 on Friday, also started uneasily, letting his approach at the first slide off into the swale on the right of the green.

It was an untidy bogey and the Spaniard admitted to hitting another poor approach at the 13th, although that did not cost a shot. And while he was quick to explain afterwards how hard the set-up had been for the third round, Rahm kept battling away. Although he fell seven strokes behind at one point, he birdied three of the last seven holes for a 68. "Two under is a much better round than I thought it was for a while," said the US Open champion. "It could have been a shot better, given myself a better chance if I had avoided

that bogey on the first, but besides that it was a pretty good round of golf."

Rahm finished at seven under par, five behind at the end of the day but he would still be a looming presence for the final round. Conners got in one better at eight under par. The 29-year-old from Ontario missed the cut on his only previous appearance in The Open in 2019 but since then had begun picking up valuable major experience. He finished in the top 10 at the last two Masters Tournaments and led on the first day of the PGA Championship at Kiawah Island.

Getting through the tricky opening stretch — the first six holes on Saturday were among the top-nine hardest for the day — Conners collected four birdies in five holes at the start of the back nine. On a course beginning to firm up after a few days of sunshine and wind, the Canadian's quietly impressive ball-striking was rewarded as he hit 13 of 14 fairways and 16 out of 18 greens in regulation.

"I felt I struck it really well today," Conners said. "I could have had a stretch of making birdies anywhere throughout the round if I could have got some putts to fall. I had a few more good chances coming in." Conners had nipped in front of his compatriot Mackenzie Hughes by one and ended the round tied

A stop-start day for Jon Rahm until he went three under for the last seven holes.

It's a
FACT

Since The Open was extended to 72 holes in 1892, only seven players have led outright after each of the first three rounds and gone on to win. The last to do so was Rory McIlroy in 2014. Previously, the feat was achieved by Ted Ray, 1912; Bobby Jones, 1927; Gene Sarazen, 1932; Henry Cotton, 1934; Tom Weiskopf, 1973; and Tiger Woods, 2005.

for fourth place with Scottie Scheffler, who birdied the last, almost holing his approach shot, for a 69.

Dylan Frittelli also birdied the last to salvage a 70. He was playing with his college teammate, Spieth. It was Frittelli who claimed the decisive point that led the University of Texas to the 2012 NCAA Championship. The South African is probably more often used to playing second fiddle to the three-time major champion and now was no different. On those challenging opening holes, Spieth made his move in his own inimitable fashion.

From the rough at the second hole, he hit his second to two feet. He holed a long putt at the fourth and, after dropping one at the fifth, hit his tee shot at the sixth to four feet. A long eagle attempt at the seventh almost fell but with his fourth birdie of the day Spieth tied for the lead with Oosthuizen.

In contrast, Morikawa found the early going a trial. He found a bunker at the first and holed from eight feet for a par. At the next he found a trap off the tee and hit his third to the back of the green. He had to hole a second putt of four feet for the bogey. At the third he got up and down. At the fourth he missed a chance and then came the fifth, where his tee shot landed near a

Collin Morikawa took a tumble in a bunker at the fifth.

Willett cameo raises English hopes

One of the talking points at the start of the week centred on the fact that you had to go back to Sir Nick Faldo in 1992 to find the last Englishman to lift the Claret Jug — and to Tony Jacklin in 1969 at Lytham & St Annes to do so in England.

Perhaps this would be the year to end the drought, on a course appropriately bearing the name of England's patron saint.

The first round certainly offered hope. Five Englishmen finished within three strokes of the lead on three under par — Justin Rose, Danny Willett, Tommy Fleetwood, Andy Sullivan and Jack Senior — while Paul Casey was just one shot further back.

By the end of the third round, however, English dreams were effectively being shelved for another year. There had been moments to savour, but not enough to mount a sustained challenge to those atop the leaderboard.

Take Willett, for instance. Could there have been a more joyous sight than when the 2016 Masters champion holed out from 124 yards at the par-4 10th for an eagle? That took him to six under par and into the top 10, just five shots off the lead. In a year in which he caught Covid-19 and then needed surgery for appendicitis and a hernia, it was much needed relief. His barely controlled laughter spoke volumes.

Yet it is a game of highs and lows. At the 14th, Willett could only watch in despair as his tee shot flew out of bounds to the right and onto Prince's next door.

Suddenly it seemed as if the English challenge might have run its course. It had.

South Africa's Dylan Frittelli scored 70 alongside college teammate Spieth.

Brooks Koepka's chances set sail with a 72 on Saturday.

"Louis Oosthuizen is known as Shrek because of his gap-toothed grin and the golfing world could be about to witness Shrek 2 – after half a dozen false starts in the production process."

—David Facey,
The Sun on Sunday

"So many questions remain after a giddying third round in which so much happened and so little actually changed."

—James Corrigan,
The Sunday Telegraph

"The pin positions — rather than the weather — proved to be the greatest defence at Royal St George's on a day when the wind didn't get above 10 mph."

—Steve Douglas,
Associated Press

"An hour after he had finished his third round, with the light fading across Sandwich Bay, Jordan Spieth was still on the practice putting green. A round that had exuded promise and kept him in the running for a second Open title had faltered at the last."

—John Westerby,
The Sunday Times

"Those playing on the second match off the first tee in the third round don't normally attract much attention. But Bryson DeChambeau is no normal golfer."

—John Huggan,
The Mail on Sunday

Oosthuizen's birdie at the 16th hole.

EXCERPTS FROM THE PRESS

"How far back is too far back? Well that depends on who you are. If there was one man Oosthuizen did not want to see in the pursuing pack at Royal St George's it was Jon Rahm."

—Neil Squires,
Sunday Express

"Give that man a hand. The galleries certainly did. With the kind of thrilling finishing flourish that grandstands were invented for, Robert MacIntyre trundled in a raking putt of some 60-feet on Royal St George's 18th green to earn a closing birdie and a rapture of applause."

—Nick Rodger,
The Herald

"Sixteen golfers from the host nation made it past Friday's cut and a number were in good nick. Across the duration of a sun-drenched third round, however, their fortunes ran high then ebbed away. Are dashed hopes as inevitable as the tides?"

—Paul MacInnes
The Observer

"Maybe it is because the home challenge melted away soon after the first ray of sunshine. Maybe it is because the fans are aware of his struggles, or his lovely victory speech from 2017 still resonates, or because he comes across as an all-round decent guy. Whatever the reason, Jordan Spieth has been adopted as one of our own. There would be no more popular winner."

—Andy Dunn,
Sunday People

A 68 for Mackenzie Hughes, who slipped behind Conners as low Canadian.

Rory McIlroy made an early charge going out in 31 but faltered coming home.

Jordan Spieth tied for the lead in the third round but bogeyed the last two holes to fall three behind Oosthuizen.

pot bunker on the left. To address the ball, Morikawa was on the edge of the bunker and, in playing his second shot, he lost balance and fell back into the sand. He was fine, but his ball was sailing towards the out of bounds fence on the right, finishing in deep rough. Another bogey, his second of the day. He had dropped only two shots over the first two days, but his fourth of the Championship was to be his last.

"I wasn't hitting that poor of golf shots," he contended. "They just weren't turning out great."

Oosthuizen was seemingly continuing on his way. A couple of chances slipped by at the first two holes; at the next two he got up and down. A 4 at the seventh reestablished his lead and he holed from 18 feet at the ninth to be out in 33. Leading by two.

Ahead, Spieth birdied the 10th to get to 12 under par, one behind. But that was his high point. As with the previous day, the American slightly faded over the closing stretch. At the 11th he failed to get up and down from a bunker, and at the 14th he took three putts from short of the green, a chance wasted. The birdies had dried up. Then came the bogeys at the last two holes. Back to nine under par, three behind, having played himself out of featuring in the final pairing on Sunday. As with Rahm, there would be belief and determination for the following day, but had he left too much to do?

Oosthuizen's poor run started at the same hole as for Spieth, the par-3 11th. He came up short, not in the same bunker but nearby. His chip was only marginally heavy-handed but a shot was lost. Two holes later, from the rough at the 13th, he came up short again and failed to get up and down. Once again he was only tied for the lead. At the next, a poor second with a 4-iron — "a horrible swing" — finished left of the green and he could not make a 4. Even a well-oiled machine can get marginally off. At the 15th, he missed the green with a 5-iron, but this was more a mental than a physical error. "I should have backed off, I thought it was the wrong club," he said. "I hate making wrong decisions. I don't mind hitting bad shots, but wrong decisions is something I have control over."

This time Oosthuizen buried the 10-footer for par. Ship righted. He hit a wedge to seven feet on the 16th and made his 2. At 12 under par, he finished on a total of 198. "I was at 13 under at one stage," he said. "Probably a good back nine I could have got to 14 or 15 under. I had a lot of opportunities to go two or three better, but I made a few bad swings in the middle of the round and that put me in some awkward positions. That's what this golf course can do to you.

"There's still lots of golf left," he concluded.

Watching alongside was Morikawa, in only his eighth major as a professional but gaining experience quickly. After his own early wobble, which had put him four shots behind, the Californian made his 4 at

> **❝** *I feel comfortable in this position. It's a lot of fun. The fans here have been great. Just enjoying the experience and having fun playing good golf.* **❞**
> —**Corey Conners**

> **❝** *I don't know if on TV you could appreciate it, but those are some of the hardest pin locations collectively I've ever seen.* **❞**
> —**Jon Rahm**

> **❝** *Sort of a tale of two nines. I played great on the front. The back nine played tough. They're sort of tucking the pins away.* **❞**
> —**Rory McIlroy**

> **❝** *Playing with Rory, the crowd was fantastic. They were cheering us on the whole way. The front nine, Rory was lighting it up a bit, so the crowd were really getting behind him. Apart from the score, I loved every minute of it.* **❞**
> —**Richard Bland**

> **❝** *I've enjoyed that Claret Jug for two years, and I'd dearly love to have it again. If it's not this year, hopefully again down the road.* **❞**
> —**Shane Lowry**

> **❝** *Obviously, as things stand I am well behind where I want to be with the leaders. It is just about trying to finish the best I can now. I have got a chance to beat my best Open Championship finish.* **❞**
> —**Matt Fitzpatrick**

> **❝** *The margin for error around here is pretty small. Unfortunately, it was one of those days where for the most part if I hit a bad shot I got hammered.* **❞**
> —**Ryan Fox**

Round of the Day: *Robert MacIntyre*

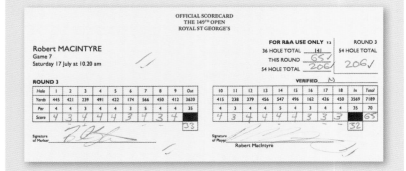

Hollow birdie for Bob

That swale on the left of the 18th green has not always been kind to Scots. Almost a century ago, George Duncan took three to get down and missed out on a play-off against Walter Hagen. In 1985, Sandy Lyle duffed a chip in Duncan's Hollow, but still ended up lifting the Claret Jug.

For Robert MacIntyre, however, bogey turned to birdie from the same dreaded spot as he holed a 60-foot putt up and across the green. It gave the 24-year-old from Oban a 65, the best score of the third round.

"Obviously that was a bonus at 18," said the only Scot in the field. "You are not expecting to hole that. You are just trying to get down in two. But my putting pace was great all day. I managed to put good pace on it, had a decent line and it went in."

MacIntyre, known as Bob, finished tied for sixth on his Open debut at Royal Portrush in 2019 but would have departed early from Sandwich without holing a 10-foot putt at the last hole on Friday to qualify on the cutline. That enabled him to launch a charge up the leaderboard, with birdies at the last two holes putting him in with the chance of a high finish on Sunday.

"Even the first two days I felt it was a strong performance," he said. "I just couldn't putt. We did some work last night and it seemed to help my confidence, just kept it rolling today. Hopefully, I can just keep doing what I'm doing."

the seventh, then holed from 30 feet for another birdie at the eighth. Another long putt fell his way at the 13th, before two putts did the business at the 14th. With his fourth birdie of the round, Morikawa was into a tie for the lead with Spieth and Oosthuizen. That made what Oosthuizen did over the next couple of holes more impressive, and Spieth over the last two more shocking.

As for Morikawa, he continued hitting fairways and greens, and was unfortunate that at least one of the chances of picking up a birdie over the last four holes did not drop.

The young star did not have many past experiences to draw on, but winning the 2020 PGA Championship at Harding Park was one. "The biggest thing I can draw from the PGA is just knowing that I can get it done," he said. "But I think confidence comes from hitting good quality shots and seeing putts go in. There is a lot to draw from, especially this week."

Morikawa believed, too. "It's going to be a gruelling 18, but I look forward to it," he added. "It's the position you want to be in. As an athlete, a golfer, you want to be in this position. I love it, so I really look forward to tomorrow."

THIRD ROUND LEADERS

HOLE	1	2	3	4	5	6	7	8	9	OUT	10	11	12	13	14	15	16	17	18	IN	TOTAL
PAR	4	4	3	4	4	3	5	4	4	35	4	3	4	4	5	4	3	4	4	35	70-210
Louis Oosthuizen	4	4	3	4	4	3	4	4	3	33	4	4	4	5	5	4	2	4	4	36	69-198
Collin Morikawa	4	5	3	4	5	3	4	3	4	35	4	3	4	3	4	3	4	4	4	33	68-199
Jordan Spieth	4	3	3	3	5	2	4	4	4	32	3	4	4	4	5	4	3	5	5	37	69-201
Corey Conners	4	4	3	4	4	3	5	4	4	35	3	3	3	3	4	3	4	4	4	31	66-202
Scottie Scheffler	4	5	3	4	4	3	4	4	4	35	4	3	4	4	5	4	3	4	4	34	69-202
Jon Rahm	5	4	2	4	4	2	6	4	4	35	4	4	3	4	4	4	3	3	4	33	68-203
Mackenzie Hughes	4	4	3	4	4	3	4	4	4	34	4	4	4	5	4	4	2	4	4	34	68-203
Dylan Frittelli	4	4	3	4	4	2	4	4	4	33	4	4	4	5	5	3	5	3	4	37	70-203
Cameron Smith	3	4	3	4	4	2	4	4	4	32	5	4	4	4	5	3	4	3	4	36	68-204
Justin Harding	4	3	3	4	4	3	5	4	4	34	4	4	4	5	4	4	4	4	3	36	70-204
Marcel Siem	4	4	3	4	4	3	4	4	4	35	3	3	4	4	8	4	2	4	3	35	70-204

■ EAGLE OR BETTER   ■ BIRDIES   □ PAR   ■ OVER PAR

SCORING SUMMARY

THIRD ROUND SCORES

Players Under Par	24
Players At Par	10
Players Over Par	43

LOW SCORES

Low First Nine
Rory McIlroy — 31

Low Second Nine
Corey Conners — 31

Low Round
Robert MacIntyre — 65

THIRD ROUND HOLE SUMMARY

HOLE	PAR	YARDS	EAGLES	BIRDIES	PARS	BOGEYS	D.BOGEYS	OTHER	RANK	AVERAGE
1	4	435	0	6	51	17	2	1	4	4.234
2	4	417	0	11	44	18	4	0	5	4.195
3	3	245	0	8	48	17	1	3	3	3.260
4	4	494	0	6	59	11	1	0	8	4.091
5	4	417	0	6	54	16	1	0	6	4.156
6	3	164	0	9	55	12	1	0	9	3.065
7	5	572	1	22	47	6	1	0	17	4.792
8	4	462	0	10	56	10	1	0	11	4.026
9	4	417	0	4	62	10	1	0	7	4.104
OUT	35	3,623	1	82	476	117	13	4		35.922
10	4	410	1	15	48	11	2	0	12	3.974
11	3	242	0	3	46	27	1	0	2	3.338
12	4	392	0	18	52	7	0	0	16	3.857
13	4	437	0	12	50	14	1	0	10	4.052
14	5	538	1	41	31	2	1	1	18	4.532
15	4	501	0	2	46	26	3	0	1	4.390
16	3	165	0	13	59	5	0	0	15	2.896
17	4	422	0	14	56	7	0	0	14	3.909
18	4	449	0	18	45	12	2	0	12	3.974
IN	35	3,556	2	136	433	111	10	1		34.922
TOTAL	70	7,179	3	218	909	228	23	5		70.844

Morikawa plays his approach to the 18th green

Oosthuizen on the verge again

Art Spander on the former Champion still leading the way after day three

This time he was familiar. A decade ago, 11 years to be exact, when virtually out of nowhere Louis Oosthuizen won The Open at St Andrews, he was such a surprise, was so little known, The R&A put out a fact sheet of his history and, of course, the pronunciation of the last name.

By The 149th Open he had become famous. To some, infamous.

While people still had trouble with the name (it's Whust-hy-zen) they knew he had become golf's "nearly man", finishing second six times in the majors.

He had been a runner-up at least once in each of the four, and in that position in the two immediately preceding this Open, the PGA Championship and the US Open. Coming close can be both a promise — the understanding you were a swing or two away — and if it happens repeatedly, an unending subject of the post-round media conferences, a curse.

Golfers are among the most honest, and most wary, of athletes or sportsmen. The scorecard offers the ultimate commentary.

There may be reasons, explanations. But if you shot 64-65 for a total of 129 on the first two days, a record, as did Oosthuizen, and then with more difficult pins a 69 on the third, to be 12 under par, you didn't need to explain much, except the obvious.

He was on the verge again.

The thinking is it's difficult to be in front after the third round, much less after all first three rounds. Yes, Oosthuizen, the South African, has a swing described as peerless, but the expectations can be overwhelming when you're reminded of all the near-misses.

In closing that third round of The 149th Open, Oosthuizen wobbled a bit before a birdie on 16. "It felt like it was a Sunday afternoon really when I made the putt and I was taking the lead," Oosthuizen said about the cheers.

It wasn't, however. He still had a round to play.

"I had a few loose swings," he said, not unusual out of 18 holes. Nobody ever played the perfect round, not Bobby Jones, Ben Hogan, Jack Nicklaus, Tiger Woods. Could-haves, would-haves, are the words of

Another fine example of Louis Oosthuizen's peerless swing as he attempted to replicate his victory in 2010 (right).

heartbreak in sport. The saddest words, we've been told, are "might have been". This was The Open. Not a club invitational. Conditions were wonderful. The R&A was going to do what was needed to make the golfers do what they needed — work hard.

"You can't really go for the pins," said Oosthuizen of the set-up, "You had to make those 20-footers for birdies."

Meaning that putting is important, as it is at every major. Back in the dawn of time — or was it the early 1930s? — someone said, "Drive for show; putt for dough." Getting the ball into the cup is what it's about, from 20 feet or 20 inches.

It was inevitable Oosthuizen would be asked how he planned to end that streak of second places. His answer was logical. "Go one better," he said. "You know, finishing second isn't great. So I will play my heart out tomorrow and see if I can lift the Claret Jug again."

When he lifted it in 2010, there was

wind and rain, the competition left far behind. Oosthuizen won by seven shots. The game seemed so simple then, if not so easy. But time moves on. Competitors such as Collin Morikawa, Jordan Spieth and Jon Rahm were not yet on tour.

Still, the strategy and tactics remain the same. Hit the ball as far and straight as you're able, keep away from those huge bunkers, or get out cleanly if you do go in, hole the putts.

Oosthuizen said at one point during The Open that he didn't get upset about a bad shot, just about bad planning before the shot.

"A lead," he said, "is not like you can hang tight and just hit a few shots coming in. You need still to play proper golf and place the ball really well to avoid bogeys."

Not much different from any tournament, any round. Keep the ball in play and keep making as many putts as possible.

Oosthuizen is a likeable, down-to-earth family man who responded to his runners-up "slam" at the majors by lip-synching to Andra Day's "I'll Rise Up", a viral sensation. He is never happier, perhaps, than when he is riding one of his tractors on his farms in Florida or South Africa.

So when he was asked on Saturday night if he was a believer in fate, if after all the "almost", the close calls, the golf gods owed him something, Oosthuizen had an instant reply.

"No, no, no," he said, "it's just golf."

FOURTH ROUND
18 July 2021

Morikawa the Magnificent

By Andy Farrell

It was relentless. It was seemingly nerveless. And it was magnificent.

Collin Morikawa produced a display that was all that and more to win The 149th Open at Royal St George's. It was a performance of which any of the greats whose names were already inscribed on the Claret Jug would have been proud, let alone a 24-year-old Californian playing an Open Championship links for the first time.

In so doing, Morikawa became the first male golfer to win on his debut at two different major championships. His rise in the game has been almost vertical. It was barely more than two years since he had graduated with a degree in business from the University of California-Berkeley. Less than a year before he won the PGA Championship at Harding Park. "We knew he was the one," said runner-up Paul Casey. "Instant maturity. He stamped his authority."

Now Morikawa became the 10th player to win The Open on debut and the first since Ben Curtis at the same venue in 2003. Ben Hogan, Tony Lema and Tom Watson are the only other Champions to have done it in the last six decades. He was the fourth player from America to win The Open before the age of 25 after Bobby Jones, Tiger Woods and Jordan Spieth, the runner-up here.

This was his eighth major appearance. The last player to win twice within that span at the start of their career was Jones in 1926. He is keeping good company. It was said of the great amateur: "For a man who exerted so compelling a magnetism over American sports fans, Jones was an exceptionally restrained performer. He did not dramatise himself like Hagen."

The moment Collin Morikawa became Champion Golfer of the Year.

So, too, Morikawa, who plays with a calm, constrained demeanour. It never shifted as he first slipped past overnight leader Louis Oosthuizen, with a sparkling run of three birdies in a row to close the front nine, and then held off the late charges of Spieth and Jon Rahm on the way home. He won by two strokes from Spieth, and by four from Rahm and Oosthuizen, but it was not until he was left with the simplest of tap-ins to complete the victory that his obvious joy was unmasked. The gallery at the 18th green roared their approval, and took to him even more after receiving the Claret Jug and speaking in such an easy, genuine yet eloquent manner.

"To finally get to play in an Open Championship for the first time," he said, "and to win it, it's even more special. To hear 'Champion Golfer of the Year' ... chills."

Obvious, perhaps, in hindsight, and the young star did enter the week as the world number 4, but Morikawa exhibits the key skills from many past Champion Golfers from St George's. His ball-striking is highly regarded amongst modern players and fits in with a pantheon that includes Sandy Lyle, the last of the great one-iron hitters, Henry Cotton, the greatest striker of a golf ball Henry Longhurst ever saw, and Harry Vardon. JH Taylor, the first Sandwich Champion, said of Vardon, twice a winner at St George's: "He hit the ball in the centre of every club with greater frequency than any other player." As did Morikawa once he had switched his irons following the tournament in Scotland the previous week.

Not only did Morikawa hit the ball like Vardon, he putted like Bobby Locke. This was more of a surprise given a weakness on the greens that has seen him employ a number of different putting styles. Here he settled for convention from long range, and the saw

grip for the shorter ones. It worked. On Sunday, he never missed a key putt. "It felt as solid as it's going to get," he said, "especially inside 10 feet. I think in a major, on a Sunday, in contention, I wasn't thinking about anything other than making a putt. I know I can putt well in these pressure situations."

It is a priceless gift, embracing the opportunity to hole a crucial putt or hit a vital shot at the right time. "You have to be excited about these opportunities, especially coming down the stretch. I embrace those moments because I truly love what I do. I live off the adrenalin. The nerves push you to be better.

"I'm glad I look calm," he added, "because the nerves are definitely there. But you channel those nerves into excitement and energy. You can't worry about the score. Especially the last nine holes, Jordan was making birdies, I think Rahm was pushing, Louis had an amazing birdie on 11. I had to worry about every shot. Can I execute every shot to the best of my ability? Some we did, some we didn't, then you move on."

Such discipline explains how Morikawa was able to unlock the secrets of St George's on a first viewing. "There was not one shot out there that was similar to any shot I've ever hit in my life," he said.

It took Bryson DeChambeau four days, and this was not his first rodeo, to go from blasting into the rough to reining himself in and posting an early 65 on Sunday. Morikawa sets about dissecting a course with a scalpel, not a bludgeon.

"I came out this week not worried about playing against anyone else, I was just trying to learn the golf course," he said. "Learning a links style golf course is tough because there's so many slopes, and I like to know everything. I like to know every little detail possible, but it's hard to do that out here. So you have to be precise about everything. That's a challenge I looked forward to."

It worked out so well that his caddie, JJ Jakovac, could celebrate his 39th birthday with a beverage from the Claret Jug.

As the leaders set off (left), Paul Casey finished as leading Englishman (above).

It's a
FACT

Eight players entered the final round with the chance of completing four rounds under 70. For the first time, three players in one Championship achieved the feat. Collin Morikawa joined Greg Norman, from Royal St George's in 1993; Nick Price, 1994; Tiger Woods, 2000; Henrik Stenson, 2016; and Jordan Spieth, 2017 as Champions with four scores in the 60s, while Spieth and Mackenzie Hughes also completed their set. Spieth and Ernie Els are the only players to have done it twice, although Els won on neither occasion.

EXCERPTS FROM THE PRESS

"It's Collin with two Ls. And now two Ws. Collin Morikawa made golf history Sunday by becoming the first player to win two different major championships on his first try."

—Sam Farmer,
Los Angeles Times

"He hit the ball like Jack Nicklaus and putted like Tiger Woods."
—Bob Harig,
ESPN.com

"Not only did Morikawa round off his Championship tilt without a single dropped shot, he threw in four birdies for good measure, each of them impeccably timed to derail Jordan Spieth's momentum."
—Oliver Brown,
The Daily Telegraph

"As the sole Scot in the field, MacIntyre had the entire nation chewing their fingernails. For one brief moment fans harboured thoughts he might actually win the most famous trophy in golf."

—Lesley McKerracher,
Oban Times

"One of the last gestures performed by Shane Lowry in the dying minutes of his reign as Champion was to high-five a young boy on his walk from the 17th green to the 18th tee box. Thereafter, his play up the closing hole was, step by step, acclaimed by the fans crammed into the horse-shoe grandstand."
—Philip Reid,
The Irish Times

Jon Rahm came up just short (above), as Morikawa kept holing putts (right).

Robert MacIntyre was the leading British player after a dramatic weekend charge.

Another of the early 65s came from Brooks Koepka, but the four-time major winner knew it was not enough after the mistakes of Saturday. He was pipped to fifth place by Dylan Frittelli on nine under par, but shared sixth with Canada's Mackenzie Hughes. Among those one stroke further back were Dustin Johnson and Robert MacIntyre, whose merry charge was halted by a ball hit onto Prince's at the 14th.

Shane Lowry, the 2019 Champion Golfer, got a rousing reception at the last as he finished 12th, while there was time for Marcel Siem to make one more birdie at the final hole, make several more fist pumps, and leave everyone once more with a smile. It was a good day for Germany with Matthias Schmid holding off Yuxin Lin for the Silver Medal, but Schmid's playing partner, Lee Westwood, completed his 88th victory-less major, an unenviable record. Best of the English was Paul Casey in 15th alongside Siem and Corey Conners.

But four players separated themselves from the rest, as they had all year in the majors. Across the four of them in 2021, US Open winner Rahm finished at 24 under par, Morikawa and Oosthuizen were 19 under par, and Spieth 16 under par.

That is not how the final order shuffled out at Sandwich, where the final round began with Oosthuizen leading by one from Morikawa, by three from Spieth, with Rahm five back. The last Champion to lead outright after every round was Rory McIlroy in 2014. Oosthuizen had led after the second and third rounds at St Andrews in 2010 before winning by seven strokes. It was the same date, 18 July, but 11 years on the South African could not extend his fine form for one more day. While Morikawa, Spieth and Rahm all scored 66s, Oosthuizen closed with a 71.

A first shot went at the fourth, where he missed the green on the right, and as Morikawa opened with all pars, the pair were tied. Spieth appeared to have a hangover from his bogey-bogey finish the previous night. He had also bogeyed the fourth and "fatted", his word, his tee shot into a bunker at the sixth, to drop another.

It was at the par-5 seventh — down by the seaside on what was the warmest and stillest summer's day so far — that the drama started. Spieth rolled in a triple-breaking 20-footer for an eagle which "took the lid off the hole" for him. He birdied the ninth and the 10th to get to 11 under par.

Behind him, the seventh also spurred Morikawa into gear. "It was definitely a turning point," the American said. His second shot came up just short of the green and, after toying with putting it, he chipped delightfully, his ball cresting the last tier and finishing

Brooks Koepka climbed the leaderboard with an early 65.

Shane Lowry salutes the gallery at the end of his Open reign.

Left-handed amateur Yuxin Lin, from China, was pipped to the Silver Medal by Germany's Matthias Schmid.

Swashbuckling Schmid claims Silver Medal

When Matthias Schmid looks down the list of previous winners of the Silver Medal awarded to the leading amateur at The Open, he will find himself in exalted company.

The 23-year-old German joined Tiger Woods, Jose Maria Olazabal, Justin Rose and Rory McIlroy, to name but a few, in claiming one of golf's most coveted prizes. To say it was well deserved would

be an understatement.

A back-to-back winner of the European Amateur Championship in 2019 and 2020, Schmid made history in the second round by equalling the lowest score by an amateur at The Open. His swashbuckling five-under-par 65 equalled Tom Lewis's performance in 2011, coincidentally also at Royal St George's.

With scores of 71 and 72 over the weekend, to go with a first-round 74, Schmid's total of 282 left him four clear of China's Yuxin Lin (69-72-74-71), the only other amateur to make the halfway cut.

"It's something special to play well here as an amateur," Schmid said. "I guess it doesn't happen too often, so I'm very happy that I could do it this week.

"The finish on Friday was obviously huge. I was nervous, but I kept it together. I played solid and had a couple of lucky breaks at the end. I'm happy to stand here with the Silver Medal."

The highlight of Schmid's final round came at the par-5 seventh, where he was able to match playing partner Lee Westwood's eagle. A sign of things to come? It would take a brave person to bet against it.

Louis Oosthuizen's second shot at the seventh would finish in the bunker short right of the green, leading to a bogey.

next to the hole for a tap-in birdie. Oosthuizen, however, leaked his second into a bunker on the right and then made contact with too much ball, and too little sand, with his next. It hurtled over the green and finished in the back of a bunker on the other side. That one he did well to get anywhere on the green but it was a long two-putt for a bogey. Two-shot swing. "That got the round started," Morikawa said.

It was the perfect moment for Morikawa to come up with one of his best swings, a cut seven-iron approach to the eighth. "As flush as it gets," he said. The ball flirted with the hole and stopped four feet away. Another birdie. At the ninth, he made it three in a row with a putt from 22 feet. Out in 32, he was now leading by three at 14 under par. As on many British beaches, once the tide turned, it happened quickly.

Now Morikawa had to hold it together. Twice he found tricky spots on the back nine, the first of them down the bank on the right of the 10th green. The chip was good, the putt, from 12 feet for a par, even better.

Oosthuizen still had a flash of sweet-swinging genius in him and it came when his tee shot at the 253-yard 11th, the hardest hole on the course on Sunday, hit the flagstick, echoing Sir Nick Faldo's shot at the same hole in 1993 as the Englishman tried to chase down Greg Norman. The South African claimed

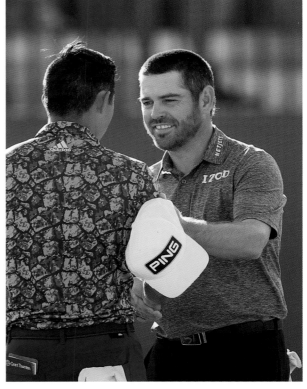

Pipped again, Oosthuizen congratulates the new Champion Golfer.

It was not all plain sailing for Morikawa on the final day, here having to save par from below the 10th green.

A solo fifth place finish for South African Dylan Frittelli.

A final fist pump at the 18th hole for Marcel Siem.

One way to get a view of the final-round drama.

A hot Sunday meant the water stations were popular.

a birdie, but at the next saw a good chance lip out and then he drove into a bunker at the 13th, costing another shot.

By now, Spieth had birdied the 13th and 14th holes to get to 13 under par and within one of Morikawa. And Rahm, who had earlier eagled the seventh but otherwise struggled to get any momentum going, was on a run that provided powerful theatre, the something extravagant he promised, but was just too late in the day. Four birdies in a row started at the 13th,

from four feet. Then he muscled his way onto the 14th green in two and two-putted, before holing from 20 feet at the 15th and hitting his tee shot at the 16th to a foot. He finished with two pars to come home in 31, a tie for third place enough to take him back above Johnson at the top of the world rankings.

Back at the par-5 14th, Oosthuizen drove into the rough but then hit his third shot to within six inches of the hole. The pressure was on Morikawa, for he knew Spieth was only one back. His second shot came up

Saturday night upset for Spieth

Jordan Spieth had no doubt where he lost The 149th Open. "The finish yesterday," he said of the bogey-bogey conclusion to his third round, "was about as upset as I've taken the finish of a round to the house. I walked in and said, 'Is there something I can break?' I knew that was so important because I would have been in the final group."

After Spieth won The Open at Royal Birkdale in 2017, his third major title, the 27-year-old from Dallas was in the final pairing on Sunday at Carnoustie the following year, but his form then took a dip. He won early in 2021 and, after finishing third at the Masters in April, showed he was back as a major contender by taking runner-up honours at Royal St George's.

Although it was Collin Morikawa who came through to win, Spieth would have preferred to play alongside leader Louis Oosthuizen on Sunday. "You feel in control when you're in the final group," he said. "You are not worried about someone going low behind you. It's a lot nicer when things are happening in front of you. When you're the last to come in, you've got the last chance on 18."

Having already had a lengthy session on the putting green after his Saturday round, Spieth said it took until after dinner to throw off his frustration. "What good does it do to be upset? You should be leading the tournament, but now I got to come out today and play with a chaser's mentality, which can be with a bit more freedom."

A second dropped shot of the day for Jordan Spieth at the sixth hole ...

... but his challenge finally got under way with an eagle at the seventh.

"Morikawa's march to victory at Royal St George's was beyond impressive. He emitted the same vibe that he did last year at Harding — poised, unflappable, determined."

—Ron Kroichick,
San Francisco Chronicle

"The next time Morikawa misses the centre of the clubface will be the first time."

—Rex Hoggard,
Golf Channel

"Morikawa is a young man in a hurry, and on Sunday, he again proved that experience was overrated, winning The Open on his first attempt. Spieth could not manage to close the gap despite all the spring in his step and urgency in his words as he talked to his shots in midair."

—Christopher Clarey,
The New York Times

"Jon Rahm finished tied-third but returned to world number 1. He finally caught fire on a scorching day with four consecutive birdies on the back nine but his 66 saw him finish four shots behind the winner."

—Neil McLeman,
Daily Mirror

"In an era where power and distance seem to determine so much, Morikawa is a throwback. His mid-iron dispersion ranges are the same as his rivals produce with wedges."

—Ewan Murray,
The Guardian

Morikawa's approach at the 72nd hole.

Round of the Day: Collin Morikawa

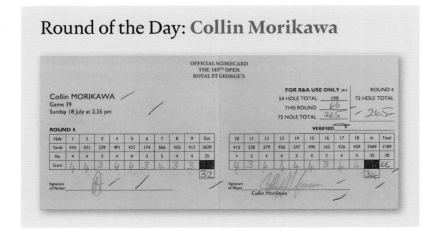

short and left of the green, but his chip did not make it up the ridge to the tier where the hole was situated. It was a 20-footer up the slope and he hit it a wee bit too hard, yet it went in. "I never thought it would," Morikawa said. "I stole one there."

Now 15 under par, Morikawa faced his next test when his approach at the 15th took a hard bounce into the rough to the left of the green. Again, it was a fine escape on to the green; again, it was an even better putt to keep the chasers at bay.

"I needed a break," said Spieth, "and I didn't get it from him. It's hard to be upset after the start. I couldn't really have done much more after being two over after six. I'm proud of going six under for the last 12 holes and putting some pressure on Collin. I played well enough to win. It was a fun battle."

Spieth and Oosthuizen parred the last four holes when they needed more; Morikawa did the same and it was more than enough. The Champion did not drop a shot on the last day, nor over the final 31 holes.

For Oosthuizen it was a fourth top-three finish in the last six majors. It is just golf, but golf can be heart-rending at times. "It was just frustrating and disappointing," said the 2010 Champion Golfer a few days later. "I knew my game was definitely there to have a good, solid day. Collin played the way you should play to win a major, especially on a Sunday. He didn't make many mistakes and when he did make a mistake, he made unbelievable up and downs for pars."

Spieth's total of 267 matched Norman's winning total from 1993 and had only been bettered by Henrik Stenson's 264 at Royal Troon in 2016 and by

Morikawa savours the walk to the final green but only began to celebrate after tapping in for his par (right).

Morikawa is congratulated by his caddie JJ Jakovac (left) before raising the Claret Jug during his victory speech (above).

Morikawa's 265 here. "Clearly, with the shots he's hit and the putts he's holed," added the 2017 Champion Golfer of the 2021 Champion Golfer, "he's not afraid of high pressure situations and winning a major championship. It's really impressive considering it's his first Open Championship and he spent a year and a half playing in an essentially crowdless environment. It's harder with big crowds. It's a bigger stage."

There is none bigger than The Open, and even with a slightly reduced gallery size, it felt every inch an Open experience to test the best players in the world.

Morikawa, who won the 2020 PGA Championship when only a few family members and coaches were allowed on site and then won a World Golf Championship in February in front of a minimal crowd, begged to differ on the theory that he still

needed to prove himself in a more normal setting. "I had nothing to prove to myself today," he said. "I hope the thing is off the table that I can play with fans and that I can play well on a Sunday."

After an enforced sabbatical for the game's oldest major, Morikawa's magnificent performance — to set alongside Vardon against Massy, Don Moe's visitation from the Lord at the Walker Cup, Cotton and his 65, Norman's conquest over Faldo et al — had provided us with an Open Championship to savour once more. He was equally appreciative.

"You look around," he said of the scene after he had tapped in on the 18th green, "and every seat is taken, everywhere is packed, those are the moments you embrace and remember. That's what is going through my head, just enjoying that moment."

FOURTH ROUND LEADERS

HOLE	1	2	3	4	5	6	7	8	9	OUT	10	11	12	13	14	15	16	17	18	IN	TOTAL
PAR	4	4	3	4	4	3	5	4	4	35	4	3	4	4	5	4	3	4	4	35	70-280
Collin Morikawa	4	4	3	4	4	3	4	3	3	32	4	3	4	4	4	4	3	4	4	34	66-265
Jordan Spieth	4	4	3	5	4	4	3	4	3	34	3	3	4	3	4	4	3	4	4	32	66-267
Jon Rahm	4	5	3	4	4	3	3	5	4	35	4	3	4	3	4	3	2	4	4	31	66-269
Louis Oosthuizen	4	4	3	5	4	3	6	4	4	37	4	2	4	5	4	4	3	4	4	34	71-269
Dylan Frittelli	4	4	4	4	4	2	4	4	4	34	3	5	4	4	5	3	3	3	4	34	68-271
Brooks Koepka	4	4	3	4	4	2	3	4	3	31	4	3	3	4	5	4	3	4	4	34	65-272
Mackenzie Hughes	5	5	2	5	3	3	4	4	4	35	3	3	3	4	5	5	3	4	3	34	69-272
Dustin Johnson	3	4	4	5	4	3	4	4	4	34	3	3	4	4	4	5	3	4	3	33	67-273
Robert MacIntyre	3	5	3	3	4	4	4	3	4	33	4	3	3	3	6	4	3	4	4	34	67-273
Daniel Berger	4	4	3	5	4	3	4	5	4	36	3	3	4	4	3	4	3	3	5	32	68-273
Scottie Scheffler	5	4	3	5	4	3	4	5	4	37	5	3	4	3	4	4	3	4	4	34	71-273

■ EAGLE OR BETTER   ■ BIRDIES   □ PAR   ■ OVER PAR

SCORING SUMMARY

FOURTH ROUND SCORES

Players Under Par	35
Players At Par	10
Players Over Par	32

CHAMPIONSHIP SCORES

Rounds Under Par	169
Rounds At Par	66
Rounds Over Par	230

LOW SCORES

Low First Nine

Brendan Steele	31
Brooks Koepka	31

Low Second Nine

JC Ritchie	31
Justin Rose	31
Jon Rahm	31

Low Round

Rickie Fowler	65
Bryson DeChambeau	65
Xander Schauffele	65
Brooks Koepka	65

FOURTH ROUND HOLE SUMMARY

HOLE	PAR	YARDS	EAGLES	BIRDIES	PARS	BOGEYS	D.BOGEYS	OTHER	RANK	AVERAGE
1	4	437	0	12	53	12	0	0	9	4.000
2	4	417	0	6	58	12	1	0	7	4.104
3	3	227	0	6	51	20	0	0	4	3.182
4	4	500	0	10	44	21	2	0	3	4.195
5	4	416	0	4	62	8	2	1	6	4.143
6	3	183	0	8	63	6	0	0	11	2.974
7	5	561	8	41	23	5	0	0	18	4.325
8	4	461	0	8	49	20	0	0	5	4.156
9	4	403	0	17	50	9	1	0	13	3.922
OUT	35	3,605	8	112	453	113	6	1		35.000
10	4	403	0	14	53	8	2	0	11	3.974
11	3	253	0	2	54	20	1	0	1	3.260
12	4	385	0	20	53	4	0	0	16	3.792
13	4	451	0	20	49	7	1	0	14	3.857
14	5	554	1	37	31	8	0	0	17	4.597
15	4	496	0	7	49	19	2	0	2	4.208
16	3	155	0	15	58	4	0	0	14	2.857
17	4	420	0	10	58	8	1	0	9	4.000
18	4	457	0	10	51	16	0	0	8	4.078
IN	35	3,574	1	135	456	94	7	0		34.623
TOTAL	70	7,179	9	247	909	207	13	1		69.623

66 *Always say it, I never give up, no matter how far I'm behind. You just never know what is going to happen.* 99
—**Robert MacIntyre**

66 *It's been great. The more I play this course, the more I like it. I think it is a really good test of golf.* 99
—**Viktor Hovland**

66 *Definitely a missed opportunity. Didn't play good enough on Saturday. Doesn't really matter what I finished today, I didn't have a chance to win. That's disappointing.* 99
—**Brooks Koepka**

66 *I love the emotions. I'm very grateful for everybody who was cheering for me. It's a bit embarrassing, maybe, because I'm not the winner of the tournament.* 99
—**Marcel Siem**

66 *It's just disappointing I could not continue in the same way with the blade as I did the first two days. C'est la vie.* 99
—**Andy Sullivan**

66 *Just had a bad stretch of golf yesterday, swing got a little funky, hit some poor shots, and that knocked me out of the tournament.* 99
—**Dustin Johnson**

66 *It's magic. There is nothing like The Open, and playing at the weekend is everything you imagined. As a kid growing up, it's everything you dreamed of.* 99
—**Marcus Armitage**

66 *It's going to take time for me to learn the whole ins and outs of Open golf. I don't think I'll ever figure it out, but hopefully one year I'll get the right breaks going for me.* 99
—**Bryson DeChambeau**

66 *Bogey-free again, second time in the week. It's always nice. I really enjoyed the experience. Everything is great here.* 99
—**Benjamin Hebert**

CHAMPIONSHIP HOLE SUMMARY

HOLE	PAR	YARDS	EAGLES	BIRDIES	PARS	BOGEYS	D.BOGEYS	OTHER	RANK	AVERAGE
1	4	445	0	65	293	92	14	1	7	4.125
2	4	421	0	37	319	97	10	2	4	4.185
3	3	239	0	42	312	103	5	3	5	3.172
4	4	491	0	53	307	92	13	0	6	4.140
5	4	422	0	29	321	100	13	2	2	4.222
6	3	174	0	87	333	42	1	2	14	2.925
7	5	566	13	127	254	62	9	0	17	4.843
8	4	450	0	77	319	68	1	0	12	3.985
9	4	412	0	77	305	75	6	2	9	4.037
OUT	**35**	**3,620**	**13**	**594**	**2,763**	**731**	**72**	**12**		**35.632**
10	4	415	1	79	305	71	7	2	10	4.022
11	3	238	0	24	328	107	6	0	3	3.204
12	4	379	2	111	300	50	2	0	15	3.869
13	4	456	0	74	286	102	2	1	8	4.075
14	5	547	9	240	176	27	10	3	18	4.566
15	4	496	0	28	265	158	13	1	1	4.342
16	3	162	1	94	344	26	0	0	16	2.849
17	4	426	1	79	329	54	2	0	13	3.951
18	4	450	0	80	305	72	8	0	11	4.017
IN	**35**	**3,569**	**14**	**809**	**2,638**	**667**	**50**	**7**		**34.895**
TOTAL	**70**	**7,189**	**27**	**1,403**	**5,401**	**1,398**	**122**	**19**		**70.527**

A Champion Golfer to remember

John Hopkins says Collin Morikawa impressed both on and off the course at Sandwich

For all the purity of his striking, the calmness of his bearing and the sorcery he demonstrated with his putting, it may be that the new Champion Golfer of the Year left Sandwich having made an enormous impression in another rather unexpected area. With a microphone in his hand and a smile on his face in the late afternoon sun, Collin Morikawa spoke as beautifully as he had played the preceding 72 holes of golf.

He commanded the presence of those around the green and the millions watching on television as if he was topping the bill in Las Vegas. If this was his last act at Royal St George's as Champion before he returned to the United States, then this is what many will remember him for. Rarely has a Champion been so sure-footed in their victory speech.

Opens at St George's are seldom run of the mill. Often, they are distinctive. There have been two previously in this millennium. Ben Curtis, a countryman of Morikawa's, won in 2003. Ranked 396th in the world at the start of the week he became the most unexpected Champion since the Second World War at the end of it. Curtis, 26, at the time had never been to Britain, never played a links course nor competed in a major championship. The last man previously to win a major championship at his first attempt was Francis Ouimet, the amateur, at the 1913 US Open.

Darren Clarke, the Northern Irishman, was 42 when he triumphed in 2011. If ever a man was built not to be blown over on a links, it was Clarke. Barrel-chested and well over six feet tall, he grew up playing links courses. Difficult and quirky to some, they were meat and drink to him. His victory earned him an editorial in *The Times* newspaper. True to form his celebration lasted for weeks.

It is not denigrating Curtis's and Clarke's triumphs to say their victories at Sandwich were the high points of their golfing lives. The same cannot be said of Morikawa's triumph, merely that it is a high point so far. He was ranked fourth in the world when he arrived in Kent and he had won the 2020 PGA Championship. At 24 he was considered by some to be among the best iron players in the game. "I think winning one major can happen to a lot of people playing really good golf in one week," Jordan Spieth, the 2017 Champion Golfer, said. "I think winning two, three or more … Collin has

proved that this is the stage where he wants to be."

Morikawa became the first man since the amateur Bobby Jones nearly one century earlier to have achieved a victory in two of his first eight starts in major championships, as well as being one of eight players to have won two major championships before their 25th birthday. He was averaging one victory in every ten tournaments on the PGA Tour. Credentials such as these make it foolish to say anything other than Morikawa is at the start of a career that is already stellar and could become significantly more so in time. Remember, he was still an amateur as recently as May 2019. Also remember that he lasted for all four rounds in the first 22 events he played as a professional on the PGA Tour.

Morikawa goes about his business in a way that is exemplary and worth studying. He is thoughtful and careful, not easily rattled. "I don't think I ever showed up at a golf course, at least as a professional, and hated the golf course," he said. "I always try and fit my game into how I play my best golf and I feel like I can win if I stick to what I've been doing."

Champions become champions because for that week at least they make golf seem easy. Morikawa appears to take the stress out of a stressful game all the time. He has an iron game that is stronger than steel and a swing that, to quote Spieth again, "makes it very difficult for him not to start the ball at the target." After coming 71st in the tournament in Scotland in the week before The Open, he changed three of his irons to get back the feeling that was missing when he hit the ball.

It is said that his only weakness is his putting and he is prone to changing his grip according to the distance from the flagstick. The greens were running at 10 or so on a Stimpmeter, which is probably significantly slower than Morikawa is used to. It didn't matter. He thought about what was required of him on the putting surfaces in Scotland, then in the south of England, and worked it out so well that he went 31 holes without a bogey and he didn't three-putt once at St George's.

"Everything about my stats says I'm not a good putter statistically," Morikawa said on the Sunday of his victory. "I feel like I can get a lot better. But in these situations I feel everything is thrown off the table. Forget about all your stats … it is who can perform well in these situations."

At Sandwich, Morikawa certainly did.

The 149th Open

Complete Scores

Royal St George's, Sandwich, England · 15-18 July 2021

HOLE	POS		1	2	3	4	5	6	7	8	9	10	11	12	13	14	15	16	17	18			TOTAL
PAR			4	4	3	4	4	3	5	4	4	4	3	4	4	5	4	3	4	4			
Collin Morikawa	T9	Rd1	4	4	2	4	5	2	5	3	4	4	3	4	4	5	4	2	4	4	67		
USA	2	Rd2	3	4	3	4	3	3	5	3	3	4	2	3	4	4	5	3	4	4	64		
$2,070,000	2	Rd3	4	5	3	4	5	3	4	3	4	4	3	4	3	4	4	3	4	4	68		
	1	Rd4	4	4	3	4	4	3	4	3	4	3	4	4	4	4	4	3	4	4	66	-15	**265**
Jordan Spieth	T2	Rd1	4	4	4	4	3	2	4	3	4	4	3	4	4	5	3	2	4	4	65		
USA	3	Rd2	3	3	4	3	4	3	5	4	4	3	3	3	4	5	5	3	4	4	67		
$1,198,000	3	Rd3	4	3	3	3	5	2	4	4	4	3	4	4	4	5	4	3	5	5	69		
	2	Rd4	4	4	3	5	4	4	3	4	3	3	3	4	3	4	4	3	4	4	66	-13	**267**
Jon Rahm	T74	Rd1	4	4	3	4	5	2	5	4	6	4	3	4	4	5	4	3	4	3	71		
Spain	T12	Rd2	4	4	3	4	4	2	4	4	3	4	3	4	3	4	3	3	4	4	64		
$682,500	T6	Rd3	5	4	2	4	4	2	6	4	4	4	3	4	4	4	3	3	4	4	68		
	T3	Rd4	4	5	3	4	4	3	3	5	4	4	3	4	3	4	3	2	4	4	66	-11	**269**
Louis Oosthuizen	1	Rd1	4	4	3	4	4	3	5	3	3	3	3	4	3	4	4	2	4	4	64		
South Africa	1	Rd2	3	4	3	4	4	3	4	4	4	4	3	3	3	3	4	4	4	4	65		
$682,500	1	Rd3	4	4	3	4	4	4	4	4	4	4	4	4	5	5	4	2	4	4	69		
	T3	Rd4	4	4	3	5	4	3	6	4	4	4	2	4	5	4	4	3	4	4	71	-11	**269**
Dylan Frittelli	T4	Rd1	4	4	3	4	4	4	4	3	4	4	2	4	4	4	4	3	3	4	66		
South Africa	T4	Rd2	5	4	3	4	4	3	5	4	4	3	3	4	4	4	4	2	3	4	67		
$480,000	T6	Rd3	4	4	3	4	4	2	4	4	4	4	4	4	5	5	3	5	3	4	70		
	5	Rd4	4	4	4	4	4	2	4	4	4	3	5	4	4	5	3	3	3	4	68	-9	**271**
Brooks Koepka	T32	Rd1	4	5	3	4	3	3	5	4	3	4	3	4	4	4	4	3	4	5	69		
USA	T12	Rd2	4	3	4	6	3	3	4	4	3	4	3	4	4	4	5	2	3	3	66		
$386,500	T25	Rd3	4	5	4	5	3	4	4	4	4	4	3	4	4	4	4	4	4	4	72		
	T6	Rd4	4	4	3	4	4	2	4	4	3	4	3	3	4	5	4	3	4	4	65	-8	**272**
Mackenzie Hughes	T4	Rd1	4	4	3	3	3	2	5	4	4	3	3	3	4	5	5	3	4	4	66		
Canada	T12	Rd2	4	3	4	4	4	3	4	4	5	4	3	4	4	4	4	3	4	4	69		
$386,500	T6	Rd3	4	4	3	4	4	3	4	4	4	4	4	4	5	4	4	2	4	3	68		
	T6	Rd4	5	5	2	5	3	3	4	4	4	4	3	3	4	5	5	3	4	3	69	-8	**272**
Dustin Johnson	T19	Rd1	4	4	2	4	3	3	5	5	5	4	2	4	4	4	3	4	4	4	68		
USA	T4	Rd2	4	4	4	4	3	3	4	3	4	4	3	3	3	4	5	3	4	3	65		
$255,250	T18	Rd3	4	4	3	5	4	3	6	5	4	5	4	4	4	4	2	4	4	4	73		
	T8	Rd4	3	4	4	5	4	3	4	3	4	3	4	4	4	5	3	4	3	4	67	-7	**273**

(A) Denotes amateur

HOLE		1	2	3	4	5	6	7	8	9	10	11	12	13	14	15	16	17	18		
PAR	POS	4	4	3	4	4	3	5	4	4	4	3	4	4	5	4	3	4	4		TOTAL
Robert MacIntyre	T91 Rd1	4	4	3	5	4	3	5	5	5	4	3	4	4	5	4	2	4	4	72	
Scotland	T65 Rd2	3	5	3	4	5	3	5	4	4	4	3	4	4	4	4	3	4	3	69	
$255,250	T18 Rd3	4	3	4	4	4	3	4	3	4	4	3	4	4	4	4	3	3	3	65	
	T8 Rd4	3	5	3	3	4	4	4	3	4	4	3	3	3	6	4	3	4	4	67	-7 **273**
Daniel Berger	T48 Rd1	4	4	3	4	4	2	5	4	4	5	3	4	4	4	5	3	4	4	70	
USA	T25 Rd2	4	4	3	4	4	3	4	3	3	4	3	4	4	5	4	3	4	4	67	
$255,250	T12 Rd3	4	4	4	4	4	3	5	4	4	4	2	3	4	5	4	2	4	4	68	
	T8 Rd4	4	4	3	5	4	3	4	5	4	3	3	4	4	3	4	3	3	5	68	-7 **273**
Scottie Scheffler	T9 Rd1	4	4	2	4	4	3	4	4	4	5	4	4	3	4	4	3	3	4	67	
USA	T4 Rd2	4	5	3	4	4	3	4	4	3	3	3	3	4	4	4	3	4	4	66	
$255,250	T4 Rd3	4	5	3	4	4	3	4	4	4	4	3	4	4	5	4	3	4	3	69	
	T8 Rd4	5	4	3	5	4	3	4	5	4	5	3	4	3	4	4	3	4	4	71	-7 **273**
Viktor Hovland	T19 Rd1	3	4	3	4	5	3	5	4	3	3	3	4	4	4	4	3	4	5	68	
Norway	T40 Rd2	5	4	3	5	4	3	5	3	4	4	2	4	4	5	5	3	4	4	71	
$181,083	T33 Rd3	4	3	3	4	5	4	5	4	3	4	3	3	4	4	6	3	4	3	69	
	T12 Rd4	4	4	3	3	4	3	4	4	4	4	3	4	4	4	4	3	4	3	66	-6 **274**
Emiliano Grillo	T48 Rd1	5	4	3	4	4	3	5	4	4	4	4	4	4	4	4	3	3	4	70	
Argentina	T7 Rd2	4	3	3	5	3	2	6	4	4	3	4	3	3	4	4	3	3	3	64	
$181,083	T18 Rd3	4	3	6	4	4	2	5	4	4	4	4	4	4	5	4	3	4	4	72	
	T12 Rd4	5	4	3	4	4	3	3	4	4	4	3	4	4	4	5	2	3	5	68	-6 **274**
Shane Lowry	T74 Rd1	5	5	3	4	4	2	5	4	4	4	4	3	4	5	5	2	3	5	71	
Republic of Ireland	T17 Rd2	4	3	3	4	5	2	5	3	3	4	3	4	4	5	3	3	3	4	65	
$181,083	T12 Rd3	4	4	3	5	4	3	4	4	5	4	3	3	5	5	4	2	3	4	69	
	T12 Rd4	4	4	3	4	4	2	4	5	3	5	3	4	4	4	5	3	4	4	69	-6 **274**
Tony Finau	T48 Rd1	4	4	2	4	4	3	5	4	4	4	3	5	3	4	4	3	4	6	70	
USA	**T17 Rd2**	4	4	2	4	3	3	5	3	3	5	3	5	4	4	3	3	4	4	66	
$143,063	T33 Rd3	4	4	4	3	4	3	6	4	4	4	4	4	3	4	5	3	4	5	72	
	T15 Rd4	4	3	3	3	5	3	4	3	5	4	3	4	3	5	3	4	4	4	67	-5 **275**
Paul Casey	T19 Rd1	3	4	2	4	4	3	5	4	4	4	3	4	4	5	4	3	4	4	68	
England	**T12 Rd2**	4	5	3	4	4	3	4	3	3	5	3	3	4	4	4	3	4	4	67	
$143,063	T12 Rd3	5	4	3	4	3	3	5	4	4	4	4	4	4	5	4	3	3	4	70	
	T15 Rd4	4	4	3	4	4	3	5	4	4	4	4	4	3	5	4	3	4	4	70	-5 **275**
Marcel Siem	T9 Rd1	4	4	3	4	4	3	6	3	3	4	3	3	5	4	4	2	4	4	67	
Germany	**T7 Rd2**	4	4	4	4	4	3	5	3	4	4	3	4	4	4	4	3	3	3	67	
$143,063	T9 Rd3	4	4	3	4	4	3	5	4	4	3	3	4	4	8	4	2	4	3	70	
	T15 Rd4	4	4	3	5	4	3	5	4	4	4	4	4	4	5	4	3	4	3	71	-5 **275**
Corey Conners	T19 Rd1	3	4	3	3	6	2	5	4	4	4	2	4	4	4	5	3	4	4	68	
Canada	**T17 Rd2**	4	4	4	4	4	3	5	4	4	4	3	4	4	3	4	2	4	4	68	
$143,063	T4 Rd3	4	4	3	4	4	3	5	4	4	3	3	3	3	4	4	3	4	4	66	
	T15 Rd4	5	5	3	4	4	2	3	5	4	4	3	5	4	5	5	3	4	5	73	-5 **275**
Sergio Garcia	T19 Rd1	4	4	3	3	5	2	5	3	4	4	3	5	4	5	5	3	3	3	68	
Spain	**T25 Rd2**	4	5	3	4	5	3	5	3	3	3	3	4	4	4	5	3	3	5	69	
$109,000	T44 Rd3	3	6	4	4	3	3	5	5	4	4	3	4	4	5	5	3	4	4	73	
	T19 Rd4	4	3	3	4	4	3	4	5	4	3	3	4	3	4	4	3	4	4	66	-4 **276**
Brandt Snedeker	T19 Rd1	3	4	4	4	4	3	5	4	4	4	3	4	5	5	4	2	2	4	68	
USA	**T17 Rd2**	3	4	4	4	6	3	6	4	3	4	2	3	4	4	4	3	4	3	68	
$109,000	T33 Rd3	5	4	4	4	5	4	5	4	3	4	3	4	5	4	4	3	4	3	72	
	T19 Rd4	4	4	3	4	3	3	4	5	4	4	3	4	5	4	4	3	4	3	68	-4 **276**

HOLE			1	2	3	4	5	6	7	8	9	10	11	12	13	14	15	16	17	18			
PAR	**POS**		4	4	3	4	4	3	5	4	4	3	4	4	5	4	3	4	4	4			**TOTAL**
Brian Harman	T2	Rd1	3	3	2	4	3	3	5	3	5	4	3	5	3	5	4	3	4	3	65		
USA	T17	Rd2	4	5	4	4	5	2	4	3	5	5	3	4	5	4	4	2	4	4	71		
$109,000	T25	Rd3	4	3	3	5	5	2	5	4	4	4	3	5	3	5	5	3	3	5	71		
	T19	Rd4	3	4	3	4	4	3	5	5	3	4	4	5	4	4	5	2	4	3	69	-4	**276**
Aaron Rai	T48	Rd1	5	4	3	3	5	2	6	4	4	4	3	4	3	5	4	3	4	4	70		
England	T40	Rd2	4	4	3	4	4	3	5	4	4	4	3	4	4	5	4	3	4	3	69		
$109,000	T25	Rd3	4	3	3	4	4	3	5	3	4	4	3	4	3	5	5	3	4	4	68		
	T19	Rd4	4	5	4	5	4	3	4	4	4	3	3	4	4	4	4	2	4	4	69	-4	**276**
Webb Simpson	T4	Rd1	4	4	2	3	4	3	6	4	4	4	3	3	4	4	4	2	4	4	66		
USA	T31	Rd2	4	4	3	5	6	3	5	4	4	3	3	3	4	6	5	3	3	4	72		
$109,000	T12	Rd3	4	5	3	4	4	3	4	3	4	4	3	4	4	4	4	3	4	3	67		
	T19	Rd4	4	5	4	3	4	3	5	4	3	5	4	3	4	4	4	3	4	5	71	-4	**276**
Kevin Streelman	T48	Rd1	3	4	3	6	3	2	5	5	4	4	3	4	5	5	4	2	4	4	70		
USA	T40	Rd2	5	4	4	4	5	3	4	3	3	4	3	4	4	5	3	3	4	4	69		
$109,000	T12	Rd3	4	4	2	4	4	3	5	4	4	3	3	4	4	4	4	3	3	4	66		
	T19	Rd4	4	4	4	6	4	3	4	4	5	3	4	3	4	4	4	3	4	4	71	-4	**276**
Justin Harding	T9	Rd1	4	4	3	4	4	2	7	3	4	4	3	4	4	4	4	2	3	4	67		
South Africa	T7	Rd2	4	4	3	3	5	3	6	4	3	3	3	4	4	3	4	3	4	4	67		
$109,000	T9	Rd3	4	3	3	4	4	3	5	4	4	4	4	4	5	4	4	4	4	3	70		
	T19	Rd4	4	4	3	5	4	3	4	4	4	4	3	5	5	4	4	3	4	5	72	-4	**276**
Xander Schauffele	T32	Rd1	4	4	3	5	4	2	5	4	4	4	3	4	4	4	5	3	3	4	69		
USA	T53	Rd2	5	4	3	6	5	3	5	4	3	3	3	3	5	4	5	3	3	4	71		
$79,821	T58	Rd3	4	4	4	4	4	3	5	4	4	4	4	5	4	4	3	4	4	4	72		
	T26	Rd4	4	3	3	4	3	4	4	3	4	3	4	3	4	4	4	3	4	4	65	-3	**277**
Byeong Hun An	T9	Rd1	3	4	3	4	4	3	4	3	4	4	3	4	5	5	4	4	3	3	67		
Korea	T25	Rd2	4	5	3	4	4	3	4	4	5	4	4	4	4	5	4	2	3	4	70		
$79,821	T44	Rd3	4	4	6	4	4	4	5	4	5	3	4	3	3	5	4	3	4	4	73		
	T26	Rd4	3	4	3	4	4	2	4	4	4	4	3	4	4	5	4	3	4	4	67	-3	**277**
Ian Poulter	T91	Rd1	4	5	3	4	4	2	5	4	4	5	3	4	5	5	4	2	4	5	72		
England	T31	Rd2	3	5	2	4	4	3	4	3	3	4	3	4	4	5	3	3	4	5	66		
$79,821	T41	Rd3	4	4	4	5	3	3	5	4	4	4	3	5	5	4	4	2	4	4	71		
	T26	Rd4	4	4	3	5	5	3	4	4	3	4	3	3	4	4	5	2	4	4	68	-3	**277**
Matt Fitzpatrick	T74	Rd1	4	4	3	5	4	3	5	4	4	5	3	4	4	5	4	3	4	3	71		
England	T53	Rd2	4	4	3	4	5	3	5	4	3	4	4	3	4	5	4	3	4	3	69		
$79,821	T25	Rd3	4	4	3	4	4	3	5	3	5	4	3	3	4	4	4	3	3	4	67		
	T26	Rd4	4	4	4	4	4	3	4	4	4	4	3	4	4	5	3	4	4	4	70	-3	**277**
Cameron Tringale	T32	Rd1	3	5	3	4	4	3	5	4	4	4	2	4	4	5	4	2	4	4	69		
USA	T12	Rd2	5	3	2	4	3	3	4	4	4	4	3	4	4	4	5	3	3	4	66		
$79,821	T18	Rd3	4	4	4	4	4	4	4	4	4	5	3	4	4	4	4	3	4	4	71		
	T26	Rd4	4	4	3	4	4	3	6	4	4	5	3	4	4	5	4	2	4	4	71	-3	**277**
Jason Kokrak	T48	Rd1	3	4	3	4	5	3	4	4	5	3	3	4	5	5	4	3	4	4	70		
USA	T53	Rd2	4	4	3	4	4	3	5	3	4	5	3	4	5	5	4	2	5	3	70		
$79,821	T18	Rd3	4	4	2	4	4	3	4	4	4	4	3	4	4	4	3	3	3	4	66		
	T26	Rd4	4	4	4	3	4	3	4	4	4	4	4	3	4	5	5	3	5	4	71	-3	**277**
Andy Sullivan	T9	Rd1	3	4	3	3	4	3	6	3	5	3	4	4	5	3	3	4	3	4	67		
England	T7	Rd2	4	4	3	3	4	3	5	4	4	4	3	3	4	4	5	2	4	4	67		
$79,821	T12	Rd3	4	4	3	4	4	3	5	4	5	4	3	3	4	5	5	4	4	3	71		
	T26	Rd4	4	4	3	4	4	3	5	4	4	4	3	4	4	6	4	3	4	5	72	-3	**277**

HOLE			1	2	3	4	5	6	7	8	9	10	11	12	13	14	15	16	17	18		
PAR	POS		4	4	3	4	4	3	5	4	4	4	3	4	4	5	4	3	4	4		TOTAL
Bryson DeChambeau	T74	Rd1	5	4	3	4	4	3	4	5	5	4	3	3	3	4	5	3	5	4	71	
USA	T65	Rd2	4	4	3	5	5	3	4	5	3	5	3	4	4	4	3	3	4	4	70	
$60,143	T64	Rd3	4	4	3	4	4	3	5	4	6	4	3	4	5	4	5	3	3	4	72	
	T33	Rd4	3	4	3	4	4	3	4	4	4	4	3	3	3	4	4	3	4	4	65	-2 **278**
Benjamin Hebert	T4	Rd1	4	4	2	3	4	3	5	4	4	4	3	4	4	4	4	3	4	4	66	
France	T53	Rd2	5	4	3	4	4	3	6	5	4	4	3	4	5	6	4	3	3	4	74	
$60,143	T53	Rd3	5	5	3	3	4	4	5	4	4	4	3	4	4	5	4	2	4	4	71	
	T33	Rd4	4	4	2	4	4	3	5	4	4	4	3	4	3	5	4	3	3	4	67	-2 **278**
Tommy Fleetwood	T9	Rd1	4	4	3	5	4	2	5	4	3	3	3	4	5	4	4	3	4	3	67	
England	T31	Rd2	4	4	3	4	4	3	5	5	5	3	3	4	4	4	4	3	5	4	71	
$60,143	T33	Rd3	4	5	2	4	4	3	4	4	4	4	3	3	4	5	6	3	4	4	70	
	T33	Rd4	4	4	3	4	5	3	4	5	4	3	4	4	3	5	4	3	4	4	70	-2 **278**
Talor Gooch	T32	Rd1	3	4	3	4	4	3	5	4	4	4	3	5	4	4	4	3	4	4	69	
USA	T65	Rd2	4	4	3	4	3	4	4	4	5	5	3	4	5	5	4	3	4	4	72	
$60,143	T33	Rd3	4	4	3	4	4	3	5	4	4	4	3	4	4	5	2	3	3	4	67	
	T33	Rd4	4	4	4	5	4	3	4	4	3	5	3	4	3	5	4	3	4	4	70	-2 **278**
Lanto Griffin	T32	Rd1	3	5	3	3	4	2	5	3	5	4	3	4	4	6	4	2	5	4	69	
USA	T40	Rd2	4	4	3	4	4	3	5	4	4	4	3	4	4	4	4	3	4	5	70	
$60,143	T25	Rd3	4	4	3	4	3	4	5	3	4	4	3	4	5	4	4	3	4	3	68	
	T33	Rd4	4	4	4	4	4	3	4	4	4	3	3	4	4	6	5	3	4	4	71	-2 **278**
Danny Willett	T9	Rd1	3	4	3	4	3	4	6	4	4	4	4	3	4	4	3	3	4	3	67	
England	T17	Rd2	4	4	4	3	4	3	4	3	4	4	4	4	4	4	5	3	4	4	69	
$60,143	T18	Rd3	4	5	3	3	4	3	5	4	2	3	4	4	4	6	5	3	4	4	70	
	T33	Rd4	4	4	4	5	4	3	5	4	4	4	3	4	4	5	4	2	4	4	72	-2 **278**
Cameron Smith	T32	Rd1	4	4	3	4	4	3	5	4	4	4	3	4	4	5	3	4	4	4	69	
Australia	T17	Rd2	5	3	4	4	4	3	5	3	3	4	2	4	4	4	5	2	3	5	67	
$60,143	T9	Rd3	3	4	3	4	4	2	4	4	4	5	4	4	4	5	3	4	3		68	
	T33	Rd4	4	4	3	5	6	2	5	4	3	6	3	4	4	6	6	3	3	3	74	-2 **278**
JC Ritchie	T74	Rd1	3	4	3	5	4	3	5	4	4	4	3	3	5	5	4	2	5	5	71	
South Africa	T65	Rd2	4	4	3	4	5	2	4	4	3	4	3	4	3	7	4	3	4	5	70	
$45,417	T64	Rd3	5	5	2	5	4	3	5	4	4	5	2	4	4	4	4	4	4	4	72	
	T40	Rd4	4	3	3	5	4	3	5	4	4	4	3	3	4	4	3	3	3	4	66	-1 **279**
Justin Thomas	T91	Rd1	4	4	3	3	4	3	5	4	5	4	3	5	4	6	4	3	4	4	72	
USA	T40	Rd2	4	3	3	4	5	3	3	4	4	4	3	4	4	5	4	3	4	3	67	
$45,417	T44	Rd3	4	4	5	4	4	2	5	4	4	4	3	4	4	5	3	4	5		71	
	T40	Rd4	4	5	4	4	4	3	4	4	4	4	3	4	3	4	4	3	4	4	69	-1 **279**
Max Homa	T48	Rd1	6	4	3	4	4	3	5	4	4	4	3	4	3	4	4	3	4	4	70	
USA	T40	Rd2	4	4	3	4	4	3	4	4	4	4	3	4	5	5	4	3	3	4	69	
$45,417	T44	Rd3	5	4	3	5	4	3	5	4	4	3	3	4	4	4	4	3	4	5	71	
	T40	Rd4	4	4	3	3	5	3	4	4	5	4	3	4	3	5	4	3	4	4	69	-1 **279**
Daniel van Tonder	T19	Rd1	5	4	3	4	3	2	5	4	3	4	3	4	4	4	4	3	4	5	68	
South Africa	T7	Rd2	4	4	3	4	5	3	5	3	4	4	3	3	4	4	4	3	3	3	66	
$45,417	T33	Rd3	4	6	4	4	4	3	6	5	4	5	3	3	3	4	4	3	4	5	74	
	T40	Rd4	4	4	3	4	4	4	5	4	5	4	3	3	4	4	4	3	4	5	71	-1 **279**
Dean Burmester	T48	Rd1	4	4	3	5	4	3	5	4	4	4	3	4	4	4	4	3	4	4	70	
South Africa	T25	Rd2	4	3	3	4	5	3	4	4	3	3	3	3	4	4	5	3	4	5	67	
$45,417	T33	Rd3	4	4	3	4	4	3	4	6	4	4	3	4	4	4	5	3	4	4	71	
	T40	Rd4	5	4	3	4	5	3	4	4	4	3	3	4	4	4	5	3	5	4	71	-1 **279**

HOLE			1	2	3	4	5	6	7	8	9	10	11	12	13	14	15	16	17	18			
PAR	POS		4	4	3	4	4	3	5	4	4	3	4	4	5	4	3	4	4	4			TOTAL
Matt Wallace	T48	Rd1	5	3	3	5	4	3	4	3	5	4	3	4	5	4	4	3	4	4	70		
England	T31	Rd2	4	4	4	4	4	3	5	4	4	3	4	3	4	4	4	2	4	4	68		
$45,417	T25	Rd3	4	5	2	4	5	5	4	3	3	4	3	3	4	4	5	3	4	4	69		
	T40	Rd4	4	4	3	3	4	3	5	5	4	4	3	4	4	4	6	3	5	4	72	-1	**279**
Jazz Janewattananond	T48	Rd1	3	5	3	4	5	3	5	4	4	4	3	4	4	4	4	3	4	4	70		
Thailand	T40	Rd2	4	4	2	3	4	3	6	4	4	4	3	4	3	5	5	3	4	4	69		
$33,679	T64	Rd3	3	4	4	4	4	3	5	4	5	4	3	5	5	4	5	3	4	5	74		
	T46	Rd4	4	4	3	4	4	3	4	4	4	4	3	4	4	4	5	2	4	3	67	E	**280**
Adam Scott	T115	Rd1	4	4	3	5	5	2	5	4	5	4	3	4	5	5	4	3	4	4	73		
Australia	T40	Rd2	4	4	3	3	4	2	4	4	4	4	3	4	4	5	4	3	3	4	66		
$33,679	T58	Rd3	4	4	3	6	3	3	5	4	4	3	4	4	5	4	3	4	4	6	73		
	T46	Rd4	3	3	4	3	5	3	4	4	4	3	4	4	4	4	4	4	3	5	68	E	**280**
Harris English	T137	Rd1	5	3	4	4	5	3	5	4	5	4	4	3	4	5	5	2	4	6	75		
USA	T53	Rd2	3	4	4	4	5	3	5	4	3	4	2	3	4	3	4	3	4	3	65		
$33,679	T58	Rd3	5	3	3	4	4	4	4	5	4	3	3	4	5	4	4	3	5	5	72		
	T46	Rd4	4	4	4	4	4	3	4	5	4	3	4	3	4	4	4	3	3	4	68	E	**280**
Johannes Veerman	T48	Rd1	4	4	3	4	4	3	6	4	4	3	3	4	5	4	4	3	4	4	70		
USA	T31	Rd2	4	4	2	4	4	2	5	4	4	3	3	5	5	4	4	2	5	4	68		
$33,679	T44	Rd3	4	5	3	4	4	3	5	4	4	3	5	3	3	5	5	3	5	4	72		
	T46	Rd4	4	4	2	3	4	3	4	4	4	4	4	5	5	4	4	3	4	5	70	E	**280**
Rory McIlroy	T48	Rd1	3	4	3	4	5	4	6	3	4	4	4	4	4	4	4	3	4	3	70		
Northern Ireland	T53	Rd2	5	5	3	3	4	3	5	4	3	4	3	3	4	5	4	4	5	3	70		
$33,679	T41	Rd3	3	4	3	3	5	2	4	4	3	4	4	5	5	5	3	4	4	4	69		
	T46	Rd4	5	4	2	5	4	3	5	4	3	6	3	3	3	5	4	4	4	4	71	E	**280**
Justin Rose	T9	Rd1	3	4	3	4	4	3	5	4	4	3	3	4	3	5	4	3	4	4	67		
England	T25	Rd2	5	5	4	4	4	3	6	4	3	4	3	3	4	3	4	3	4	4	70		
$33,679	T25	Rd3	4	4	2	5	4	3	4	4	4	4	4	4	5	4	3	4	4	4	70		
	T46	Rd4	4	4	4	4	7	4	5	5	5	4	2	4	4	4	3	2	4	4	73	E	**280**
Joel Dahmen	T32	Rd1	3	5	3	4	4	2	5	3	4	4	4	4	4	5	5	2	4	4	69		
USA	T25	Rd2	4	3	3	4	4	3	4	3	4	4	4	3	4	5	5	4	3	4	68		
$33,679	T18	Rd3	5	4	3	4	4	3	5	4	4	4	4	4	4	4	3	4	3	3	69		
	T46	Rd4	5	5	3	4	4	3	6	5	5	4	3	4	4	4	5	2	4	4	74	E	**280**
Rickie Fowler	T32	Rd1	4	4	3	4	4	3	6	3	4	4	4	4	4	4	4	3	4	3	69		
USA	T65	Rd2	4	4	3	4	4	3	5	5	4	4	3	4	5	4	5	3	4	4	72		
$29,417	T73	Rd3	4	5	4	5	4	3	5	4	4	4	5	3	5	4	4	2	5	5	75		
	T53	Rd4	5	4	2	4	4	3	3	5	3	4	3	3	3	4	3	4	4	4	65	+1	**281**
Chan Kim	T48	Rd1	4	4	3	4	5	2	5	3	4	4	3	5	4	4	4	3	4	5	70		
USA	T40	Rd2	4	5	3	4	5	3	4	4	4	4	3	3	4	4	5	3	4	3	69		
$29,417	T64	Rd3	4	5	3	4	5	3	5	4	4	5	4	4	5	5	4	3	3	4	74		
	T53	Rd4	3	4	3	4	4	3	5	4	4	3	4	5	5	4	3	2	4	4	68	+1	**281**
Billy Horschel	T48	Rd1	4	4	3	5	5	2	4	4	3	4	3	4	4	5	4	3	5	4	70		
USA	T40	Rd2	4	4	3	3	3	3	5	4	5	4	4	4	4	4	4	3	4	4	69		
$29,417	T58	Rd3	4	5	3	4	4	4	5	4	4	4	4	4	5	3	4	4	4	4	73		
	T53	Rd4	3	4	3	5	4	4	4	4	4	4	4	4	4	4	3	3	4	4	69	+1	**281**
Jonathan Thomson	T74	Rd1	5	6	4	4	4	2	5	4	5	4	3	3	3	4	5	2	4	4	71		
England	T31	Rd2	4	4	3	4	4	3	5	3	4	4	3	5	4	4	5	1	3	4	67		
$29,417	T53	Rd3	5	3	4	4	4	4	5	4	4	3	3	3	4	7	5	3	4	4	73		
	T53	Rd4	3	4	3	4	4	4	4	4	4	5	4	3	4	5	5	3	4	3	70	+1	**281**

HOLE			1	2	3	4	5	6	7	8	9	10	11	12	13	14	15	16	17	18	TOTAL
PAR	POS		4	4	3	4	4	3	5	4	4	3	4	4	5	4	3	4	4	4	
Marcus Armitage	T32	Rd1	4	5	3	3	4	3	6	4	4	3	3	4	4	5	4	2	4	4	69
England	T65	Rd2	4	4	4	5	4	3	6	4	4	4	3	4	5	4	4	3	3	4	72
$29,417	T53	Rd3	4	3	3	5	5	4	4	4	4	3	4	4	4	5	4	2	4	4	70
	T53	Rd4	4	4	3	4	4	3	4	4	3	4	4	3	4	6	4	3	5	4	70 +1 **281**
Christiaan Bezuidenhout	T19	Rd1	4	4	4	4	4	2	4	4	4	5	3	5	4	4	4	3	3	3	68
South Africa	T53	Rd2	3	4	4	5	4	2	5	4	3	5	3	4	5	5	5	3	4	4	72
$29,417	T44	Rd3	4	4	2	4	4	3	5	5	4	5	3	4	3	4	4	3	5	4	70
	T53	Rd4	5	4	3	3	4	3	5	4	5	4	3	4	3	5	4	3	5	4	71 +1 **281**
Ryosuke Kinoshita	T91	Rd1	4	6	5	3	4	3	4	3	5	3	3	4	5	4	6	2	4	4	72
Japan	T65	Rd2	3	4	3	4	4	3	5	4	4	5	4	4	3	4	4	3	4	4	69
$27,929	T64	Rd3	4	5	3	5	4	3	7	4	4	3	3	4	4	4	4	3	4	4	72
	T59	Rd4	4	4	3	4	4	3	4	4	4	4	3	4	4	5	4	2	5	4	69 +2 **282**
Chez Reavie	T91	Rd1	4	5	4	4	4	3	5	4	4	4	3	4	4	4	5	4	3	4	72
USA	T31	Rd2	4	4	4	3	4	3	4	4	4	4	3	4	4	4	4	2	3	4	66
$27,929	T58	Rd3	4	4	6	4	5	3	5	4	4	4	3	4	5	4	3	3	4	5	74
	T59	Rd4	4	6	3	4	4	3	4	4	3	3	3	4	5	4	5	2	4	5	70 +2 **282**
Joaquin Niemann	T32	Rd1	5	4	3	3	5	3	5	4	4	5	3	4	3	5	4	2	3	4	69
Chile	T40	Rd2	4	4	4	4	4	3	4	4	4	4	3	4	5	4	4	3	5	3	70
$27,929	T58	Rd3	5	4	3	4	5	3	6	4	4	6	3	5	4	3	4	3	4	3	73
	T59	Rd4	4	4	4	4	4	3	5	4	4	4	3	4	4	4	3	4	4	4	70 +2 **282**
Abraham Ancer	T32	Rd1	4	4	3	4	4	3	5	3	4	4	3	4	5	4	4	3	4	4	69
Mexico	T53	Rd2	4	4	3	5	5	3	5	4	4	4	3	3	5	4	5	3	3	4	71
$27,929	T53	Rd3	7	5	3	4	4	3	4	4	4	4	3	4	4	5	4	2	3	4	71
	T59	Rd4	3	4	3	4	3	3	5	3	4	4	4	4	5	5	3	5	5	4	71 +2 **282**
Bernd Wiesberger	T74	Rd1	4	4	3	5	4	2	5	5	4	4	3	4	4	4	5	3	4	4	71
Austria	T65	Rd2	4	5	3	5	5	3	5	3	3	4	3	3	5	4	4	3	4	4	70
$27,929	T53	Rd3	3	4	4	5	4	3	5	4	4	5	3	4	4	5	3	3	3	4	70
	T59	Rd4	4	5	3	4	4	2	5	5	5	4	4	3	4	4	2	5	4	4	71 +2 **282**
Lee Westwood	T74	Rd1	4	4	3	4	4	2	5	5	4	5	3	4	4	5	3	4	4	4	71
England	T31	Rd2	5	4	3	4	5	2	4	4	4	4	3	3	3	4	5	3	4	3	67
$27,929	T44	Rd3	5	4	3	4	4	3	5	3	4	5	4	4	5	5	4	3	4	3	72
	T59	Rd4	4	5	2	5	4	3	3	3	4	4	5	4	5	5	4	4	4	4	72 +2 **282**
Matthias Schmid [A]	T127	Rd1	3	4	3	4	3	3	5	4	5	4	4	4	5	5	4	4	4	6	74
Germany	T40	Rd2	4	4	3	3	4	3	5	4	4	4	3	3	4	4	4	2	3	4	65
	T44	Rd3	3	6	3	4	4	3	5	4	4	4	4	4	4	4	3	4	5	3	71
	T59	Rd4	4	4	4	4	4	3	3	5	4	5	3	4	4	5	4	3	4	5	72 +2 **282**
Antoine Rozner	T48	Rd1	3	4	3	5	4	3	4	4	5	4	3	5	4	4	5	3	4	3	70
France	T65	Rd2	5	4	3	5	4	2	5	3	4	5	3	3	4	6	5	3	3	4	71
$27,929	T33	Rd3	4	4	3	4	3	3	4	5	4	3	4	5	3	4	3	4	4	3	67
	T59	Rd4	5	5	4	4	5	3	5	4	6	3	3	3	4	5	4	3	4	4	74 +2 **282**
Brendan Steele	T115	Rd1	5	4	2	4	5	2	6	4	4	4	3	4	4	5	5	3	4	5	73
USA	T65	Rd2	4	4	3	4	4	3	5	3	3	4	3	4	4	5	4	2	4	5	68
$26,900	T71	Rd3	5	4	3	4	6	4	5	4	5	3	3	4	6	4	4	3	3	4	74
	T67	Rd4	3	4	3	4	3	3	4	4	3	4	4	4	6	4	3	4	4	4	68 +3 **283**
Richard Bland	T48	Rd1	4	5	3	4	4	3	4	4	4	4	4	4	4	4	4	2	4	5	70
England	T53	Rd2	4	4	4	5	4	3	5	4	4	4	3	5	4	4	3	3	4	3	70
$26,900	T64	Rd3	4	5	3	4	4	3	5	5	4	4	4	4	4	5	3	4	4	4	73
	T67	Rd4	4	4	3	4	4	3	4	4	3	4	5	4	3	5	4	5	3	4	70 +3 **283**

HOLE			1	2	3	4	5	6	7	8	9	10	11	12	13	14	15	16	17	18	
PAR	POS		4	4	3	4	4	3	5	4	4	4	3	4	4	5	4	3	4	4	TOTAL
Jack Senior	T9	Rd1	3	4	3	4	4	3	5	3	4	4	3	3	4	5	4	3	4	4	67
England	T31	Rd2	3	4	3	4	5	3	4	4	3	4	3	4	4	6	5	3	4	5	71
$26,900	T44	Rd3	5	4	4	3	4	3	5	4	4	4	3	5	4	5	3	3	4	5	72
	T67	**Rd4**	5	3	4	4	4	3	5	5	3	4	3	4	3	5	5	3	6	4	73 +3 **283**
Sam Horsfield	T48	Rd1	4	4	3	4	4	2	4	4	4	4	4	4	5	4	5	3	4	4	70
England	T53	Rd2	4	4	3	5	4	4	4	4	4	4	4	4	4	4	4	2	4	4	70
$26,900	T41	Rd3	4	3	4	4	5	3	3	5	5	4	3	4	3	4	5	3	4	3	69
	T67	**Rd4**	4	4	4	6	4	3	4	5	4	5	3	3	4	5	5	3	4	4	74 +3 **283**
Ryan Fox	T19	Rd1	4	3	3	5	4	3	4	4	4	3	3	4	4	6	4	2	4	4	68
New Zealand	T17	Rd2	3	5	3	4	6	3	5	4	3	4	3	3	4	5	4	3	3	3	68
$26,900	T25	Rd3	5	6	3	4	4	3	4	3	4	4	2	4	4	4	6	3	4	4	71
	T67	**Rd4**	4	4	3	5	4	3	4	5	4	4	4	4	6	6	4	3	4	5	76 +3 **283**
Padraig Harrington	T91	Rd1	6	4	3	4	3	5	3	3	3	4	4	5	5	3	3	5	4	5	72
Republic of Ireland	T53	Rd2	4	4	4	4	4	3	4	4	5	3	3	3	4	4	3	3	4	5	68
$26,375	T64	Rd3	4	4	3	4	5	3	5	3	4	5	4	4	4	4	4	3	4	6	73
	72	**Rd4**	5	4	3	5	4	3	5	5	4	4	3	3	4	5	4	3	4	3	71 +4 **284**
Kevin Kisner	T48	Rd1	3	3	3	4	4	3	6	4	5	4	3	5	4	4	4	3	4	4	70
USA	T40	Rd2	4	4	2	4	4	4	5	4	3	5	3	3	4	5	4	3	4	4	69
$26,250	T75	Rd3	6	4	3	4	5	3	6	5	5	3	4	5	5	5	3	5	3	4	78
	73	**Rd4**	3	4	3	5	3	3	6	3	4	4	3	4	4	4	4	3	4	4	68 +5 **285**
Richard Mansell	T91	Rd1	4	4	3	4	4	3	5	5	4	6	3	4	4	4	3	3	5	4	72
England	T65	Rd2	6	4	3	5	4	2	4	4	4	4	3	4	3	5	3	3	4	4	69
$26,125	T75	Rd3	5	5	3	4	4	4	5	4	5	4	3	4	3	5	5	4	4	5	76
	T74	**Rd4**	4	4	3	4	6	3	4	5	4	5	3	3	4	4	3	4	3	3	69 +6 **286**
Yuxin Lin [A]	**T32**	**Rd1**	3	4	3	4	4	3	5	3	4	5	3	3	4	4	5	3	4	5	69
China	T65	Rd2	4	4	3	5	6	3	5	4	4	3	3	3	5	4	5	3	4	4	72
	T71	Rd3	5	5	3	4	4	3	5	4	4	4	4	4	4	5	5	3	4	4	74
	T74	**Rd4**	4	4	4	5	4	2	5	3	4	4	4	4	4	5	4	3	4	4	71 +6 **286**
Poom Saksansin	T115	Rd1	5	5	3	4	4	2	5	4	4	4	3	4	5	4	5	3	5	4	73
Thailand	T65	Rd2	4	4	3	3	4	3	5	4	4	4	3	4	4	4	4	3	4	4	68
$25,938	T75	Rd3	5	4	3	4	5	2	5	5	5	5	4	4	4	6	5	2	4	4	76
	T76	**Rd4**	4	4	3	4	4	3	5	4	4	4	3	4	4	5	4	3	4	5	71 +8 **288**
Sam Burns	T74	Rd1	4	5	2	4	4	3	5	4	5	3	3	5	4	5	4	3	4	4	71
USA	T53	Rd2	4	4	4	5	4	2	5	4	4	4	3	4	4	4	3	3	4	4	69
$25,938	T73	Rd3	6	4	4	4	4	3	5	4	4	6	3	5	5	4	3	4	4	4	76
	T76	**Rd4**	4	5	3	4	5	3	6	4	4	3	3	3	4	6	4	3	3	5	72 +8 **288**

NON QUALIFIERS AFTER 36 HOLES
(Leading 10 professionals and ties receive $8,000 each, next 20 professionals and ties receive $6,500 each, remainder of professionals and ties receive $5,350 each)

HOLE			1	2	3	4	5	6	7	8	9	10	11	12	13	14	15	16	17	18	
PAR	POS		4	4	3	4	4	3	5	4	4	4	3	4	4	5	4	3	4	4	TOTAL
Harold Varner III	T48	Rd1	3	4	4	4	4	2	6	4	4	5	3	4	4	4	4	3	4	4	70
USA	**T78**	**Rd2**	4	4	4	5	4	3	6	3	5	4	3	3	5	4	4	3	5	3	72 +2 **142**
Francesco Molinari	T19	Rd1	3	5	2	4	4	3	5	4	4	4	3	5	3	4	4	4	4	3	68
Italy	**T78**	**Rd2**	3	4	4	4	4	7	4	3	6	5	4	3	4	5	4	3	3	4	74 +2 **142**
Marc Leishman	T137	Rd1	4	4	3	4	4	3	6	4	4	5	3	5	5	5	4	3	4	5	75
Australia	**T78**	**Rd2**	4	5	3	4	4	2	5	4	4	4	3	3	4	5	4	3	3	3	67 +2 **142**

HOLE		1	2	3	4	5	6	7	8	9	10	11	12	13	14	15	16	17	18			
PAR	POS	4	4	3	4	4	3	5	4	4	3	4	4	5	4	3	4	4	4			TOTAL
Sebastian Munoz	T115 Rd1	5	4	3	4	5	2	6	4	4	4	3	4	4	4	5	4	4	4	73		
Colombia	**T78** Rd2	4	4	3	5	4	3	6	4	3	4	3	4	3	4	5	3	4	3	69	+2	**142**
Keegan Bradley	T74 Rd1	5	4	3	3	4	3	5	4	4	4	4	4	4	5	5	3	3	4	71		
USA	**T78** Rd2	4	4	2	4	5	3	5	5	5	3	3	4	5	4	5	3	4	3	71	+2	**142**
Russell Henley	T48 Rd1	3	4	4	4	4	3	6	4	6	5	4	3	4	4	5	2	4	3	70		
USA	**T78** Rd2	4	5	3	4	4	3	5	4	4	4	3	4	4	5	4	3	4	5	72	+2	**142**
Tyrrell Hatton	T91 Rd1	5	4	3	5	4	3	5	4	4	4	2	4	4	4	5	3	5	4	72		
England	**T78** Rd2	4	4	3	4	4	3	5	5	3	3	5	3	4	4	4	3	5	4	70	+2	**142**
Henrik Stenson	T74 Rd1	4	5	3	4	4	2	5	4	4	4	4	4	4	4	4	3	5	4	71		
Sweden	**T78** Rd2	4	4	4	6	4	3	6	4	3	4	3	3	4	4	4	3	4	4	71	+2	**142**
Kurt Kitayama	T74 Rd1	4	4	4	4	4	2	6	5	5	4	3	3	5	4	3	4	4	4	71		
USA	**T78** Rd2	4	4	3	5	4	4	5	4	3	3	3	4	5	4	5	3	3	4	71	+2	**142**
Jimmy Walker	T48 Rd1	4	5	3	4	5	3	5	4	4	3	4	4	3	4	3	2	5	5	70		
USA	**T78** Rd2	4	4	3	4	4	4	7	3	4	5	4	5	4	4	4	2	4	3	72	+2	**142**
Rikard Karlberg	T91 Rd1	3	4	5	5	4	3	7	4	4	4	3	3	4	4	5	3	3	4	72		
Sweden	**T78** Rd2	4	4	2	3	4	3	5	4	3	5	4	4	4	5	3	4	5		70	+2	**142**
Ryutaro Nagano	T48 Rd1	4	4	3	4	4	3	5	4	4	4	2	4	5	5	3	4	4		70		
Japan	**T78** Rd2	4	4	3	4	4	3	5	5	4	5	4	3	4	5	4	3	4	4	72	+2	**142**
Ryan Palmer	T91 Rd1	4	4	4	4	4	3	5	4	4	3	3	4	4	5	5	3	5	4	72		
USA	**T78** Rd2	4	6	4	4	4	3	4	4	4	4	3	4	4	4	4	3	4	3	70	+2	**142**
Chris Kirk	T19 Rd1	3	4	3	4	4	3	5	4	4	4	2	4	5	4	4	2	4	5	68		
USA	**T78** Rd2	5	5	4	5	4	3	5	4	4	4	3	4	4	5	4	3	4	4	74	+2	**142**
Marcus Kinhult	T32 Rd1	3	4	3	4	5	2	6	5	5	4	3	4	4	4	3	3	3	4	69		
Sweden	**T78** Rd2	4	5	4	4	5	3	5	5	4	4	3	4	4	5	3	3	4	4	73	+2	**142**
Jorge Campillo	T91 Rd1	5	4	3	4	4	3	5	4	4	4	3	4	5	5	3	4	4		72		
Spain	**T78** Rd2	5	5	4	5	4	3	5	4	3	3	3	5	4	4	3	3	3		70	+2	**142**
Victor Perez	T48 Rd1	5	4	3	4	4	3	4	3	4	4	3	3	5	6	4	3	4	4	70		
France	**T78** Rd2	4	4	3	3	4	7	5	4	4	3	3	5	4	4	5	3	4	3	72	+2	**142**
Guido Migliozzi	T32 Rd1	4	4	3	3	5	2	5	4	3	4	4	4	4	4	5	3	4	4	69		
Italy	**T78** Rd2	6	4	3	4	5	3	5	4	4	4	2	4	5	3	5	3	5	4	73	+2	**142**
Martin Kaymer	T127 Rd1	4	4	3	5	4	2	5	4	4	4	3	5	5	5	5	3	5	4	74		
Germany	**T78** Rd2	4	4	3	5	4	2	5	4	3	5	3	4	4	4	4	2	4	4	68	+2	**142**
Takumi Kanaya	T48 Rd1	4	4	3	3	4	3	6	4	4	4	3	4	4	4	5	3	4	4	70		
Japan	**T78** Rd2	4	4	3	6	3	3	5	4	4	4	2	4	5	7	4	3	4	3	72	+2	**142**
Troy Merritt	T115 Rd1	4	4	3	4	4	3	5	5	5	4	3	4	3	5	4	3	5	5	73		
USA	**T98** Rd2	4	4	3	4	4	4	5	3	4	4	3	4	4	6	4	3	4	3	70	+3	**143**
Patrick Cantlay	T127 Rd1	4	5	2	4	5	2	5	4	5	4	3	3	7	4	5	2	5	5	74		
USA	**T98** Rd2	4	4	3	6	3	5	4	3	3	3	3	4	3	4	4	3	4	5	69	+3	**143**
Charley Hoffman	T91 Rd1	4	4	3	4	5	3	6	4	4	4	3	4	4	4	5	3	4	4	72		
USA	**T98** Rd2	4	4	3	4	4	4	5	4	4	4	3	3	4	6	3	5	3	3	71	+3	**143**
Rafa Cabrera Bello	T48 Rd1	4	4	2	5	4	3	5	4	4	4	4	3	5	5	4	2	4	4	70		
Spain	**T98** Rd2	5	4	3	4	5	3	5	4	4	3	4	5	5	4	5	3	3	4	73	+3	**143**
Brendon Todd	T91 Rd1	5	4	3	4	3	3	6	4	6	5	3	4	4	4	5	4	4	4	72		
USA	**T98** Rd2	4	4	3	4	4	3	5	4	4	5	3	4	4	5	4	3	4	4	71	+3	**143**
Matthias Schwab	T74 Rd1	4	4	3	3	5	3	5	4	5	4	5	4	4	4	4	3	4	4	71		
Austria	**T98** Rd2	4	5	3	4	5	3	5	5	4	4	3	4	3	5	4	3	4	4	72	+3	**143**
Shaun Norris	T91 Rd1	3	3	3	6	4	3	5	4	4	4	4	5	5	4	5	2	4	4	72		
South Africa	**T98** Rd2	4	5	3	5	4	3	5	4	4	5	2	4	3	4	5	3	4	4	71	+3	**143**

HOLE			1	2	3	4	5	6	7	8	9	10	11	12	13	14	15	16	17	18			TOTAL
PAR	POS		4	4	3	4	4	3	5	4	4	4	3	4	4	5	4	3	4	4			TOTAL
Matt Jones	T91	Rd1	4	4	4	4	4	3	5	4	4	5	4	4	4	4	5	3	4	3	72		
Australia	**T98**	Rd2	4	5	3	4	4	3	5	4	5	3	3	5	3	5	4	3	4	4	71	+3	**143**
Daniel Hillier	T91	Rd1	4	5	3	4	4	3	5	4	5	4	4	3	4	5	5	2	4	4	72		
New Zealand	**T98**	Rd2	4	4	3	4	4	2	5	4	3	4	4	5	4	7	4	2	4	4	71	+3	**143**
Patrick Reed	T91	Rd1	4	4	3	4	5	2	6	4	4	5	3	3	5	5	4	3	4	4	72		
USA	**T98**	Rd2	4	4	4	4	5	3	4	4	4	4	3	5	3	4	5	3	4	4	71	+3	**143**
Laird Shepherd [A]	T127	Rd1	4	5	3	4	4	3	5	4	4	4	5	4	5	5	4	3	4	4	74		
England	**T98**	Rd2	6	5	2	4	5	2	4	4	4	3	4	3	3	5	4	3	4	4	69	+3	**143**
Min Woo Lee	T127	Rd1	5	3	3	3	4	3	6	3	4	4	3	5	4	5	7	3	4	5	74		
Australia	**T98**	Rd2	4	4	4	4	4	3	3	4	3	5	3	4	5	4	4	3	4	4	69	+3	**143**
Gary Woodland	T115	Rd1	4	4	3	5	4	3	5	4	4	3	3	4	4	6	5	3	4	5	73		
USA	**T98**	Rd2	4	4	3	4	4	3	4	4	5	5	4	5	4	5	4	2	3	3	70	+3	**143**
Lucas Herbert	T48	Rd1	6	4	3	4	4	3	5	5	4	3	3	3	3	3	4	3	4	4	70		
Australia	**T98**	Rd2	4	5	4	4	4	3	5	4	4	5	3	4	5	4	4	3	4	4	73	+3	**143**
Branden Grace	T91	Rd1	4	4	3	4	5	3	6	4	4	6	4	4	3	4	3	3	4	4	72		
South Africa	**T98**	Rd2	4	4	3	4	4	4	3	4	8	3	3	4	4	5	4	3	4	3	71	+3	**143**
Stewart Cink	T4	Rd1	4	4	3	4	4	2	5	4	4	3	3	4	3	4	4	3	4	4	66		
USA	**T98**	Rd2	5	5	4	4	5	3	5	4	4	3	3	4	5	8	5	3	3	4	77	+3	**143**
Erik van Rooyen	T32	Rd1	4	4	3	4	4	2	5	4	4	4	4	3	4	5	4	3	4	4	69		
South Africa	**T98**	Rd2	4	4	3	4	3	4	5	4	4	4	3	5	5	5	4	3	5	5	74	+3	**143**
John Catlin	T137	Rd1	4	4	3	4	4	3	5	3	5	3	5	5	4	6	6	3	3	5	75		
USA	**T115**	Rd2	4	4	3	4	4	3	5	4	3	4	3	4	4	4	6	3	3	4	69	+4	**144**
Adam Hadwin	T137	Rd1	5	5	3	4	4	3	6	5	5	4	3	3	4	5	5	3	4	4	75		
Canada	**T115**	Rd2	4	4	2	4	5	3	4	4	4	4	2	4	5	4	6	2	4	4	69	+4	**144**
Jason Scrivener	T115	Rd1	4	3	4	4	5	2	5	5	4	4	3	4	5	5	5	3	4	4	73		
Australia	**T115**	Rd2	5	4	3	4	4	3	5	5	3	4	2	4	4	5	6	3	3	4	71	+4	**144**
Keith Mitchell	T19	Rd1	4	4	3	3	4	2	5	4	4	4	3	4	4	5	4	4	4	4	68		
USA	**T115**	Rd2	5	5	3	4	4	3	6	5	5	4	3	4	4	5	5	3	3	5	76	+4	**144**
Richard T Lee	T137	Rd1	3	4	4	4	5	4	5	5	5	4	3	4	4	6	5	2	4	4	75		
Canada	**T115**	Rd2	5	4	3	4	4	3	5	4	3	4	3	4	4	4	4	3	4	4	69	+4	**144**
Ricardo Celia	T91	Rd1	4	5	2	4	4	3	6	4	5	5	3	4	4	5	4	3	4	3	72		
Colombia	**T115**	Rd2	4	4	3	4	4	3	5	5	4	4	3	4	4	5	3	4	4	5	72	+4	**144**
Haotong Li	T137	Rd1	5	5	3	4	7	4	4	4	4	4	3	4	5	4	4	2	5	4	75		
China	**T115**	Rd2	4	4	4	4	5	2	5	4	4	3	3	4	4	5	4	3	3	4	69	+4	**144**
Mike Lorenzo-Vera	T137	Rd1	5	4	3	4	5	3	4	4	4	5	4	3	5	6	5	3	4	4	75		
France	**T115**	Rd2	5	5	3	3	3	3	5	4	3	4	2	4	4	4	5	3	4	5	69	+4	**144**
Gonzalo Fdez-Castano	T74	Rd1	4	4	3	5	4	3	6	4	4	4	3	4	5	5	4	2	4	4	71		
Spain	**T115**	Rd2	4	5	4	5	5	4	5	3	3	4	3	4	4	4	5	4	4	3	73	+4	**144**
Ernie Els	T91	Rd1	4	3	3	4	5	4	5	4	4	4	3	3	5	5	5	3	4	4	72		
South Africa	**T115**	Rd2	5	5	4	4	4	3	6	4	3	3	4	4	3	5	4	3	4	4	72	+4	**144**
Jason Day	T137	Rd1	5	5	3	4	5	3	4	4	7	4	3	4	5	4	4	3	4	4	75		
Australia	**T125**	Rd2	6	5	3	4	4	2	5	5	4	4	3	4	4	4	3	3	4	3	70	+5	**145**
Brad Kennedy	T74	Rd1	5	4	3	4	4	3	5	5	4	4	3	4	4	4	4	3	4	4	71		
Australia	**T125**	Rd2	4	4	4	4	4	4	5	4	4	3	4	4	5	4	5	3	4	5	74	+5	**145**
Carlos Ortiz	T137	Rd1	5	4	4	4	3	2	6	4	4	5	3	5	4	5	5	3	5	4	75		
Mexico	**T125**	Rd2	3	5	4	4	5	3	3	4	3	6	3	3	5	5	5	2	4	3	70	+5	**145**
Alex Noren	T127	Rd1	4	3	4	3	4	3	5	4	5	4	3	4	5	8	5	2	4	4	74		
Sweden	**T125**	Rd2	3	4	4	6	4	3	5	4	5	3	3	3	5	5	4	2	4	4	71	+5	**145**

HOLE			1	2	3	4	5	6	7	8	9	10	11	12	13	14	15	16	17	18	
PAR	POS		4	4	3	4	4	3	5	4	4	4	3	4	4	5	4	3	4	4	TOTAL
Lucas Glover	T137	Rd1	4	4	3	4	4	2	5	4	6	5	3	4	5	5	5	2	4	6	75
USA	**T125**	Rd2	4	4	3	4	4	3	4	4	4	4	3	4	4	6	4	3	4	4	70 +5 **145**
Matt Kuchar	T127	Rd1	4	5	3	4	6	3	5	4	5	4	3	4	4	4	5	3	4	4	74
USA	**T130**	Rd2	5	4	4	4	4	3	5	4	4	4	3	4	4	5	3	4	4	4	72 +6 **146**
Thomas Detry	T91	Rd1	5	4	3	4	4	3	5	4	5	4	4	4	3	4	4	2	5	5	72
Belgium	**T130**	Rd2	4	4	3	4	4	3	4	4	4	5	3	4	4	7	5	3	5	4	74 +6 **146**
Darren Clarke	T74	Rd1	5	4	3	4	4	3	4	4	4	5	3	4	5	4	4	3	4	4	71
Northern Ireland	**T130**	Rd2	4	5	3	4	4	2	6	4	5	7	4	4	4	4	3	4	4	4	75 +6 **146**
Joe Long (A)	T115	Rd1	3	4	3	5	4	2	6	4	4	4	3	4	5	5	5	2	5	5	73
England	**T130**	Rd2	4	4	3	5	4	3	4	4	5	4	3	4	3	6	6	3	4	4	73 +6 **146**
Cole Hammer (A)	T137	Rd1	5	4	3	5	4	3	5	5	4	5	4	4	4	4	4	2	6	4	75
USA	**T130**	Rd2	4	5	3	4	4	2	5	4	3	5	4	3	5	5	5	3	4	3	71 +6 **146**
Rikuya Hoshino	T127	Rd1	5	4	4	5	5	3	4	4	4	4	4	5	3	4	4	3	5	4	74
Japan	**T130**	Rd2	4	6	3	5	4	3	5	3	4	5	3	5	4	5	3	3	3	4	72 +6 **146**
Christoffer Bring (A)	T91	Rd1	4	4	3	6	4	2	5	4	4	4	3	5	5	3	5	3	4	4	72
Denmark	**T136**	Rd2	5	5	4	4	5	3	5	4	4	4	4	4	4	4	6	3	4	3	75 +7 **147**
Jaco Ahlers	T19	Rd1	5	4	3	4	3	2	6	3	5	4	3	4	3	5	4	2	4	4	68
South Africa	**T136**	Rd2	5	5	2	5	5	3	5	4	5	5	3	3	5	7	5	4	4	4	79 +7 **147**
Joost Luiten	T151	Rd1	6	4	2	5	4	3	6	4	4	4	4	4	4	6	4	4	4	4	76
Netherlands	**T136**	Rd2	4	4	3	3	5	3	4	4	4	4	4	4	4	5	4	4	4	4	71 +7 **147**
Romain Langasque	T127	Rd1	4	4	4	5	4	3	6	3	5	4	3	4	4	4	5	3	5	4	74
France	**T136**	Rd2	4	4	3	4	5	3	5	5	4	4	4	3	4	5	5	3	4	4	73 +7 **147**
Sam Bairstow (A)	T137	Rd1	5	4	3	4	4	3	7	3	5	4	3	6	5	4	5	3	3	4	75
England	**T136**	Rd2	4	4	4	4	4	2	5	4	4	4	3	5	4	5	5	3	4	4	72 +7 **147**
CT Pan	T74	Rd1	4	4	3	4	4	3	6	3	4	4	3	4	4	4	5	3	4	5	71
Chinese Taipei	**T136**	Rd2	4	4	3	4	4	3	6	4	4	5	3	5	5	7	5	2	4	4	76 +7 **147**
Paul Waring	T91	Rd1	4	4	3	4	4	3	5	4	4	4	3	5	5	4	4	3	5	4	72
England	**T142**	Rd2	6	4	3	5	6	4	5	4	3	4	5	4	3	4	4	3	5	4	76 +8 **148**
Nicholas Poppleton	T137	Rd1	3	5	4	4	5	2	5	5	4	4	4	6	4	4	4	3	4	5	75
England	**T142**	Rd2	4	4	3	4	6	3	4	4	4	5	4	4	5	4	5	3	3	4	73 +8 **148**
Garrick Higgo	T115	Rd1	5	4	3	3	5	4	5	4	4	4	4	4	5	4	3	4	4	4	73
South Africa	**T142**	Rd2	4	5	4	4	5	3	5	4	4	5	4	4	5	4	5	3	4	3	75 +8 **148**
Adam Long	T91	Rd1	5	4	4	4	5	3	5	4	4	4	3	4	3	5	5	2	4	4	72
USA	**T145**	Rd2	4	4	3	5	5	3	6	5	4	7	3	4	4	5	3	3	5	4	77 +9 **149**
Aaron Pike	T127	Rd1	4	5	3	4	4	2	7	3	4	4	4	4	4	4	4	4	5	5	74
Australia	**T145**	Rd2	5	7	3	5	5	2	6	4	3	3	3	5	4	4	4	3	4	5	75 +9 **149**
Ben Hutchinson	T153	Rd1	4	5	3	6	4	4	5	5	5	5	5	3	3	5	5	3	4	4	77
England	**T145**	Rd2	5	4	3	5	4	3	5	4	3	4	3	5	5	4	4	3	4	4	72 +9 **149**
Abel Gallegos (A)	T115	Rd1	4	4	3	4	4	4	4	4	4	5	3	4	4	7	4	3	4	4	73
Argentina	**T145**	Rd2	5	4	3	4	4	4	4	5	4	3	3	4	5	5	5	4	5	5	76 +9 **149**
Marcel Schneider	T115	Rd1	5	4	4	4	4	3	5	4	5	4	3	5	4	4	4	3	4	4	73
Germany	**T145**	Rd2	4	5	3	4	4	3	7	4	5	4	3	3	4	6	5	3	5	4	76 +9 **149**
Sam Forgan	T115	Rd1	4	5	2	5	4	3	5	5	4	4	3	4	4	4	5	4	4	4	73
England	**T150**	Rd2	6	5	3	6	4	3	6	3	4	5	3	4	4	5	5	3	4	4	77 +10 **150**
Connor Worsdall	T153	Rd1	5	4	4	4	4	4	5	4	6	3	3	4	5	4	4	3	5	6	77
England	**T150**	Rd2	5	4	4	4	5	2	5	5	4	4	4	4	5	4	4	2	3	4	73 +10 **150**
Phil Mickelson	T155	Rd1	4	4	4	5	5	3	6	4	5	4	3	4	5	5	5	4	4	6	80
USA	**152**	Rd2	4	5	3	4	4	4	5	4	4	4	2	3	5	5	5	2	4	5	72 +12 **152**

HOLE		1	2	3	4	5	6	7	8	9	10	11	12	13	14	15	16	17	18	
PAR	POS	4	4	3	4	4	3	5	4	4	4	3	4	4	5	4	3	4	4	TOTAL
Daniel Croft	T151 Rd1	4	5	4	5	6	3	5	5	4	5	3	4	5	4	4	2	4	4	76
England	**153** Rd2	4	7	3	5	4	4	6	5	4	4	4	4	5	4	3	4	4		78 +14 **154**
Yuki Inamori	T137 Rd1	5	4	3	4	5	3	7	4	4	4	3	5	5	4	5	2	4	4	75
Japan	**154** Rd2	6	5	3	5	4	3	7	4	5	5	4	4	5	5	3	5	4		81 +16 **156**
Deyen Lawson	T155 Rd1	5	6	5	4	5	3	5	3	5	4	3	5	4	7	5	3	4	4	80
Australia	**155** Rd2	6	5	5	5	5	3	4	4	4	3	3	4	4	7	5	3	3	4	77 +17 **157**
Will Zalatoris	T32 Rd1	4	4	2	3	5	4	4	3	4	4	4	2	5	5	4	2	5	5	69 **WD**
USA																				

THE TOP TENS

Driving Distance

1 **Ryan Fox** 312.3
2 Jon Rahm 308.8
3 Dylan Frittelli 308.0
4 Bryson DeChambeau 305.3
5 Scottie Scheffler 304.5
6 Brooks Koepka 304.3
7 Sergio Garcia 304.0
8 Rory McIlroy 303.5
9 Byeong Hun An 303.4
10 Dustin Johnson 301.6
45 *Collin Morikawa* 285.8

Fairways Hit

Maximum of 56

1 **Aaron Rai** 43
2 Richard Bland 42
3 Daniel Berger 41
4 Shane Lowry 40
5 Joel Dahmen 39
5 Jon Rahm 39
5 Louis Oosthuizen 39
5 Marcel Siem 39
5 Benjamin Hebert 39
5 Danny Willett 39
5 Matthias Schmid [A] 39
5 Yuxin Lin [A] 39
39 *Collin Morikawa* 34

Greens in Regulation

Maximum of 72

1 **Jon Rahm** 58
1 **Sergio Garcia** 58
3 Tony Finau 55
3 Chan Kim 55
5 *Collin Morikawa* 54
5 Shane Lowry 54
5 Paul Casey 54
5 Corey Conners 54
5 Brandt Snedeker 54
5 Billy Horschel 54
5 Matthias Schmid [A] 54

Putts

1 *Collin Morikawa* 111
1 **Ian Poulter** 111
1 **Jazz Janewattananond** 111
4 Webb Simpson 112
4 Cameron Tringale 112
6 Jordan Spieth 113
6 Dylan Frittelli 113
6 Emiliano Grillo 113
6 Cameron Smith 113
10 Brian Harman 114
10 Xander Schauffele 114

Statistical Rankings

	Driving Distance	Rank	Fairways Hit	Rank	Greens In Regulation	Rank	Putts	Rank
Byeong Hun An	303.4	9	30	65	53	12	120	42
Abraham Ancer	276.0	60	34	39	52	17	124	68
Marcus Armitage	275.6	61	35	33	50	29	121	48
Daniel Berger	281.5	50	41	3	52	17	120	42
Christiaan Bezuidenhout	281.4	51	33	53	46	64	118	26
Richard Bland	274.5	64	42	2	50	29	126	73
Dean Burmester	289.8	36	32	59	48	45	121	48
Sam Burns	293.8	24	26	74	44	74	122	53
Paul Casey	280.9	52	35	33	54	5	120	42
Corey Conners	290.5	33	37	19	54	5	120	42
Joel Dahmen	270.8	72	39	5	47	54	120	42
Bryson DeChambeau	305.3	4	26	74	49	41	121	48
Harris English	287.9	37	38	13	46	64	117	19
Tony Finau	298.6	14	35	33	55	3	124	68
Matt Fitzpatrick	280.6	54	36	25	48	45	118	26
Tommy Fleetwood	293.3	25	28	71	51	23	118	26
Rickie Fowler	283.4	48	27	73	49	40	122	53
Ryan Fox	312.3	1	20	77	52	17	125	71
Dylan Frittelli	308.0	3	32	59	50	29	113	6
Sergio Garcia	304.0	7	36	25	58	1	129	77
Talor Gooch	287.5	39	35	33	52	17	124	68
Lanto Griffin	299.5	12	37	19	50	29	119	34
Emiliano Grillo	286.0	44	32	59	49	41	113	6
Justin Harding	274.8	63	33	53	48	45	116	14
Brian Harman	274.5	64	36	25	49	41	114	10
Padraig Harrington	290.0	35	33	53	47	56	122	53
Benjamin Hebert	273.9	66	39	6	47	56	117	19
Max Homa	290.9	30	34	39	48	45	118	26
Billy Horschel	286.5	42	33	53	54	5	126	73
Sam Horsfield	299.0	13	29	69	46	64	119	34
Viktor Hovland	282.0	49	35	33	51	23	118	26
Mackenzie Hughes	286.9	40	34	39	52	17	118	26
Jazz Janewattananond	272.9	70	34	39	41	77	111	1
Dustin Johnson	301.6	10	34	39	50	29	115	12
Chan Kim	291.9	26	30	65	55	3	126	73
Ryosuke Kinoshita	261.9	76	36	25	48	45	118	26
Kevin Kisner	286.4	43	34	39	47	56	122	53
Brooks Koepka	304.3	6	36	25	53	12	120	42
Jason Kokrak	298.3	15	26	74	51	23	122	53
Yuxin Lin [A]	296.5	18	39	6	45	73	123	65
Shane Lowry	277.8	56	40	4	54	5	122	53
Robert MacIntyre	291.8	27	36	25	53	12	117	19
Richard Mansell	296.1	19	33	52	50	28	123	65
Rory McIlroy	303.5	8	34	39	47	56	117	19
Collin Morikawa	285.8	45	34	39	54	5	111	1
Joaquin Niemann	294.6	21	32	59	46	64	122	53
Louis Oosthuizen	297.1	16	39	6	53	12	116	14
Ian Poulter	273.3	67	37	19	43	76	111	1
Jon Rahm	308.8	2	39	6	58	1	122	53
Aaron Rai	277.4	57	43	1	50	29	119	34
Chez Reavie	270.9	71	38	13	47	56	119	34
JC Ritchie	273.3	67	34	39	48	45	115	12
Justin Rose	290.9	30	33	53	49	41	117	19
Antoine Rozner	275.1	62	34	39	48	45	122	53
Poom Saksansin	257.3	77	37	17	47	54	125	71
Xander Schauffele	300.0	11	28	71	46	64	114	10
Scottie Scheffler	304.5	5	37	19	51	23	116	14
Matthias Schmid [A]	291.0	29	39	6	54	5	128	76
Adam Scott	263.6	75	34	39	50	29	121	48
Jack Senior	290.3	34	38	13	47	56	119	34
Marcel Siem	263.9	74	39	6	50	29	117	19
Webb Simpson	273.3	67	30	65	46	64	112	4
Cameron Smith	286.8	41	32	59	47	56	113	6
Brandt Snedeker	280.8	53	38	13	54	5	122	53
Jordan Spieth	296.6	17	37	17	52	16	113	6
Brendan Steele	290.8	32	33	53	46	64	119	34
Kevin Streelman	294.1	23	37	19	52	17	119	34
Andy Sullivan	277.1	58	37	19	50	29	118	26
Justin Thomas	294.3	22	36	25	50	29	122	53
Jonathan Thomson	278.5	55	30	65	44	74	117	19
Cameron Tringale	285.3	46	34	39	46	64	112	4
Daniel van Tonder	291.3	28	35	33	50	29	119	34
Johannes Veerman	287.9	37	32	59	46	64	116	14
Matt Wallace	284.4	47	29	69	51	23	122	53
Lee Westwood	295.6	20	36	25	48	45	121	48
Bernd Wiesberger	276.8	59	34	39	48	45	123	65
Danny Willett	268.1	73	39	6	47	56	116	14

NON QUALIFIERS AFTER 36 HOLES

	Driving Distance	Rank	Fairways Hit	Rank	Greens In Regulation	Rank	Putts	Rank		Driving Distance	Rank	Fairways Hit	Rank	Greens In Regulation	Rank	Putts	Rank
Jaco Ahlers	283.3	87	18	35	21	121	62	107	Matt Kuchar	277.5	114	15	95	22	110	62	107
Sam Bairstow [A]	292.8	46	17	56	27	19	67	153	Romain Langasque	285.0	76	9	153	18	146	59	49
Keegan Bradley	273.0	128	13	134	24	69	61	86	Deyen Lawson	286.8	71	13	134	15	155	61	86
Christoffer Bring [A]	272.5	130	14	112	16	153	55	3	Min Woo Lee	290.3	54	17	56	25	36	61	86
Rafa Cabrera Bello	277.0	117	14	112	24	69	64	133	Richard T Lee	281.8	95	11	145	26	29	64	133
Jorge Campillo	281.5	97	18	35	23	88	63	117	Marc Leishman	288.5	61	17	56	27	19	64	133
Patrick Cantlay	293.5	41	14	112	29	4	67	153	Haotong Li	297.8	24	11	145	19	140	55	3
John Catlin	269.5	135	18	35	26	29	66	149	Adam Long	278.0	113	16	80	24	69	66	149
Ricardo Celia	296.5	33	14	112	23	88	61	86	Joe Long [A]	294.0	38	21	3	25	36	66	149
Stewart Cink	300.3	14	15	95	25	36	60	62	Mike Lorenzo-Vera	276.5	119	16	80	25	36	63	117
Darren Clarke	275.0	125	14	112	19	140	60	62	Joost Luiten	290.0	56	17	56	19	140	61	86
Daniel Croft	272.3	131	17	56	18	146	64	133	Troy Merritt	283.3	87	16	80	25	36	62	107
Jason Day	293.8	40	15	95	22	110	58	32	Phil Mickelson	277.5	114	16	80	19	140	65	142
Thomas Detry	297.8	24	11	145	18	146	58	32	Guido Migliozzi	301.3	10	16	80	23	88	60	62
Ernie Els	299.5	17	16	80	21	121	60	62	Keith Mitchell	291.5	49	18	35	24	69	63	117
Gonzalo Fdez-Castano	271.3	132	23	1	21	121	61	86	Francesco Molinari	268.8	137	17	56	27	19	61	86
Sam Forgan	275.8	121	11	145	21	121	64	133	Sebastian Munoz	278.8	109	15	95	21	121	58	32
Abel Gallegos [A]	280.0	106	10	151	18	146	61	86	Ryutaro Nagano	285.0	76	14	112	21	121	56	18
Lucas Glover	279.5	107	14	112	25	36	65	142	Alex Noren	289.8	58	18	35	23	88	62	107
Branden Grace	292.3	47	14	112	24	69	60	62	Shaun Norris	283.8	84	14	112	20	137	58	32
Adam Hadwin	274.8	126	15	95	25	36	63	117	Carlos Ortiz	276.3	120	19	19	22	110	60	62
Cole Hammer [A]	288.5	61	12	141	23	88	65	142	Ryan Palmer	296.5	33	18	35	21	121	59	49
Tyrrell Hatton	298.8	20	17	56	24	69	62	107	CT Pan	284.5	80	18	35	25	36	65	142
Russell Henley	268.0	138	20	7	25	36	63	117	Victor Perez	287.3	67	20	7	25	36	59	49
Lucas Herbert	297.3	29	13	134	19	140	56	18	Aaron Pike	278.3	111	9	153	22	110	63	117
Garrick Higgo	290.8	52	14	112	21	121	65	142	Nicholas Poppleton	297.5	28	12	141	20	137	61	86
Daniel Hillier	286.5	72	14	112	23	88	62	107	Patrick Reed	285.5	75	15	95	25	36	65	142
Charley Hoffman	283.5	85	14	112	24	69	61	86	Marcel Schneider	283.3	87	16	80	17	150	60	62
Rikuya Hoshino	281.3	99	15	95	22	110	61	86	Matthias Schwab	267.3	139	15	95	24	69	63	117
Ben Hutchinson	284.3	82	14	112	20	137	65	142	Jason Scrivener	280.3	103	17	56	22	110	58	32
Yuki Inamori	265.0	144	17	56	16	153	64	133	Laird Shepherd [A]	293.0	44	18	35	23	88	62	107
Matt Jones	285.0	76	15	95	21	121	57	23	Henrik Stenson	261.0	149	17	56	23	88	59	49
Takumi Kanaya	264.0	146	18	35	19	140	55	3	Brendon Todd	257.8	152	20	7	17	150	55	3
Rikard Karlberg	281.0	101	14	112	24	69	59	49	Erik van Rooyen	300.8	13	19	19	21	121	60	62
Martin Kaymer	287.8	64	14	112	22	110	61	86	Harold Varner III	293.0	44	20	7	23	88	61	86
Brad Kennedy	279.5	107	21	3	26	29	68	155	Jimmy Walker	283.5	85	17	56	23	88	60	62
Marcus Kinhult	290.0	56	19	19	23	88	59	49	Paul Waring	302.3	9	12	141	24	69	66	149
Chris Kirk	290.8	52	19	19	25	36	63	117	Gary Woodland	299.5	17	13	134	25	36	64	133
Kurt Kitayama	297.8	24	14	112	22	110	60	62	Connor Worsdall	303.5	7	13	134	17	150	61	86

Roll of Honour

Year	Champion	Score	Margin	Runners-up	Venue
1860	Willie Park Sr	174	2	Tom Morris Sr	Prestwick
1861	Tom Morris Sr	163	4	Willie Park Sr	Prestwick
1862	Tom Morris Sr	163	13	Willie Park Sr	Prestwick
1863	Willie Park Sr	168	2	Tom Morris Sr	Prestwick
1864	Tom Morris Sr	167	2	Andrew Strath	Prestwick
1865	Andrew Strath	162	2	Willie Park Sr	Prestwick
1866	Willie Park Sr	169	2	David Park	Prestwick
1867	Tom Morris Sr	170	2	Willie Park Sr	Prestwick
1868	Tommy Morris Jr	154	3	Tom Morris Sr	Prestwick
1869	Tommy Morris Jr	157	11	Bob Kirk	Prestwick
1870	Tommy Morris Jr	149	12	Bob Kirk, Davie Strath	Prestwick
1871	*No Championship*				
1872	Tommy Morris Jr	166	3	Davie Strath	Prestwick
1873	Tom Kidd	179	1	Jamie Anderson	St Andrews
1874	Mungo Park	159	2	Tommy Morris Jr	Musselburgh
1875	Willie Park Sr	166	2	Bob Martin	Prestwick
1876	Bob Martin	176	–	Davie Strath	St Andrews
	(Martin was awarded the title when Strath refused to play-off)				
1877	Jamie Anderson	160	2	Bob Pringle	Musselburgh
1878	Jamie Anderson	157	2	Bob Kirk	Prestwick
1879	Jamie Anderson	169	3	Jamie Allan, Andrew Kirkaldy	St Andrews
1880	Bob Ferguson	162	5	Peter Paxton	Musselburgh
1881	Bob Ferguson	170	3	Jamie Anderson	Prestwick
1882	Bob Ferguson	171	3	Willie Fernie	St Andrews
1883	Willie Fernie	158	Play-off	Bob Ferguson	Musselburgh
1884	Jack Simpson	160	4	Douglas Rolland, Willie Fernie	Prestwick
1885	Bob Martin	171	1	Archie Simpson	St Andrews
1886	David Brown	157	2	Willie Campbell	Musselburgh
1887	Willie Park Jr	161	1	Bob Martin	Prestwick
1888	Jack Burns	171	1	David Anderson Jr, Ben Sayers	St Andrews
1889	Willie Park Jr	155	Play-off	Andrew Kirkaldy	Musselburgh
1890	John Ball Jr[A]	164	3	Willie Fernie, Archie Simpson	Prestwick
1891	Hugh Kirkaldy	166	2	Willie Fernie, Andrew Kirkaldy	St Andrews
(From 1892 the Championship was extended to 72 holes)					
1892	Harold Hilton[A]	305	3	John Ball Jr[A], Hugh Kirkaldy, Sandy Herd	Muirfield
1893	Willie Auchterlonie	322	2	John Laidlay[A]	Prestwick

Bill Rogers (1981)   Sandy Lyle (1985)   Greg Norman (1993)

Year	Champion	Score	Margin	Runners-up	Venue
1894	JH Taylor	326	5	Douglas Rolland	St George's
1895	JH Taylor	322	4	Sandy Herd	St Andrews
1896	Harry Vardon	316	Play-off	JH Taylor	Muirfield
1897	Harold Hilton[A]	314	1	James Braid	Royal Liverpool
1898	Harry Vardon	307	1	Willie Park Jr	Prestwick
1899	Harry Vardon	310	5	Jack White	St George's
1900	JH Taylor	309	8	Harry Vardon	St Andrews
1901	James Braid	309	3	Harry Vardon	Muirfield
1902	Sandy Herd	307	1	Harry Vardon, James Braid	Royal Liverpool
1903	Harry Vardon	300	6	Tom Vardon	Prestwick
1904	Jack White	296	1	James Braid, JH Taylor	Royal St George's
1905	James Braid	318	5	JH Taylor, Rowland Jones	St Andrews
1906	James Braid	300	4	JH Taylor	Muirfield
1907	Arnaud Massy	312	2	JH Taylor	Royal Liverpool
1908	James Braid	291	8	Tom Ball	Prestwick
1909	JH Taylor	295	6	James Braid, Tom Ball	Cinque Ports
1910	James Braid	299	4	Sandy Herd	St Andrews
1911	Harry Vardon	303	Play-off	Arnaud Massy	Royal St George's
1912	Ted Ray	295	4	Harry Vardon	Muirfield
1913	JH Taylor	304	8	Ted Ray	Royal Liverpool
1914	Harry Vardon	306	3	JH Taylor	Prestwick

1915-1919 No Championship

Year	Champion	Score	Margin	Runners-up	Venue
1920	George Duncan	303	2	Sandy Herd	Royal Cinque Ports
1921	Jock Hutchison	296	Play-off	Roger Wethered[A]	St Andrews
1922	Walter Hagen	300	1	George Duncan, Jim Barnes	Royal St George's
1923	Arthur Havers	295	1	Walter Hagen	Troon
1924	Walter Hagen	301	1	Ernest Whitcombe	Royal Liverpool
1925	Jim Barnes	300	1	Archie Compston, Ted Ray	Prestwick
1926	Bobby Jones[A]	291	2	Al Watrous	Royal Lytham
1927	Bobby Jones[A]	285	6	Aubrey Boomer, Fred Robson	St Andrews
1928	Walter Hagen	292	2	Gene Sarazen	Royal St George's
1929	Walter Hagen	292	6	Johnny Farrell	Muirfield
1930	Bobby Jones[A]	291	2	Leo Diegel, Macdonald Smith	Royal Liverpool
1931	Tommy Armour	296	1	Jose Jurado	Carnoustie

Year	Champion	Score	Margin	Runners-up	Venue
1932	Gene Sarazen	283	5	Macdonald Smith	Prince's
1933	Denny Shute	292	Play-off	Craig Wood	St Andrews
1934	Henry Cotton	283	5	Sid Brews	Royal St George's
1935	Alf Perry	283	4	Alf Padgham	Muirfield
1936	Alf Padgham	287	1	Jimmy Adams	Royal Liverpool
1937	Henry Cotton	290	2	Reg Whitcombe	Carnoustie
1938	Reg Whitcombe	295	2	Jimmy Adams	Royal St George's
1939	Dick Burton	290	2	Johnny Bulla	St Andrews
1940-1945 No Championship					
1946	Sam Snead	290	4	Bobby Locke, Johnny Bulla	St Andrews
1947	Fred Daly	293	1	Reg Horne, Frank Stranahan[A]	Royal Liverpool
1948	Henry Cotton	284	5	Fred Daly	Muirfield
1949	Bobby Locke	283	Play-off	Harry Bradshaw	Royal St George's
1950	Bobby Locke	279	2	Roberto de Vicenzo	Troon
1951	Max Faulkner	285	2	Antonio Cerda	Royal Portrush
1952	Bobby Locke	287	1	Peter Thomson	Royal Lytham
1953	Ben Hogan	282	4	Frank Stranahan[A], Dai Rees, Peter Thomson, Antonio Cerda	Carnoustie
1954	Peter Thomson	283	1	Syd Scott, Dai Rees, Bobby Locke	Royal Birkdale
1955	Peter Thomson	281	2	John Fallon	St Andrews
1956	Peter Thomson	286	3	Flory Van Donck	Royal Liverpool
1957	Bobby Locke	279	3	Peter Thomson	St Andrews
1958	Peter Thomson	278	Play-off	Dave Thomas	Royal Lytham
1959	Gary Player	284	2	Flory Van Donck, Fred Bullock	Muirfield
1960	Kel Nagle	278	1	Arnold Palmer	St Andrews
1961	Arnold Palmer	284	1	Dai Rees	Royal Birkdale
1962	Arnold Palmer	276	6	Kel Nagle	Troon

(Prior to 1963, scores assessed against "level 4s". From 1963, pars were introduced and holes were played in 3, 4 or 5 shots.)

Year	Champion	To Par	Score	Margin	Runners-up	Venue
1963	Bob Charles	-3	277	Play-off	Phil Rodgers	Royal Lytham
1964	Tony Lema	-9	279	5	Jack Nicklaus	St Andrews
1965	Peter Thomson	-7	285	2	Christy O'Connor Sr, Brian Huggett	Royal Birkdale
1966	Jack Nicklaus	-2	282	1	Dave Thomas, Doug Sanders	Muirfield
1967	Roberto de Vicenzo	-10	278	2	Jack Nicklaus	Royal Liverpool
1968	Gary Player	+1	289	2	Jack Nicklaus, Bob Charles	Carnoustie
1969	Tony Jacklin	-4	280	2	Bob Charles	Royal Lytham
1970	Jack Nicklaus	-5	283	Play-off	Doug Sanders	St Andrews
1971	Lee Trevino	-14	278	1	Liang Huan Lu	Royal Birkdale
1972	Lee Trevino	-6	278	1	Jack Nicklaus	Muirfield
1973	Tom Weiskopf	-12	276	3	Neil Coles, Johnny Miller	Troon
1974	Gary Player	-2	282	4	Peter Oosterhuis	Royal Lytham
1975	Tom Watson	-9	279	Play-off	Jack Newton	Carnoustie
1976	Johnny Miller	-9	279	6	Jack Nicklaus, Seve Ballesteros	Royal Birkdale
1977	Tom Watson	-12	268	1	Jack Nicklaus	Turnberry
1978	Jack Nicklaus	-7	281	2	Simon Owen, Ben Crenshaw, Ray Floyd, Tom Kite	St Andrews
1979	Seve Ballesteros	-1	283	3	Jack Nicklaus, Ben Crenshaw	Royal Lytham
1980	Tom Watson	-13	271	4	Lee Trevino	Muirfield
1981	Bill Rogers	-4	276	4	Bernhard Langer	Royal St George's
1982	Tom Watson	-4	284	1	Peter Oosterhuis, Nick Price	Royal Troon
1983	Tom Watson	-9	275	1	Hale Irwin, Andy Bean	Royal Birkdale
1984	Seve Ballesteros	-12	276	2	Bernhard Langer, Tom Watson	St Andrews
1985	Sandy Lyle	+2	282	1	Payne Stewart	Royal St George's
1986	Greg Norman	E	280	5	Gordon J Brand	Turnberry

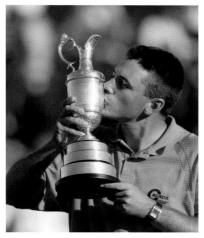

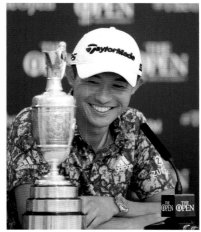

Ben Curtis (2003)   *Darren Clarke (2011)*   *Collin Morikawa (2021)*

Year	Champion	To Par	Score	Margin	Runners-up	Venue
1987	Nick Faldo	-5	279	1	Rodger Davis, Paul Azinger	Muirfield
1988	Seve Ballesteros	-11	273	2	Nick Price	Royal Lytham
1989	Mark Calcavecchia	-13	275	Play-off	Greg Norman, Wayne Grady	Royal Troon
1990	Nick Faldo	-18	270	5	Mark McNulty, Payne Stewart	St Andrews
1991	Ian Baker-Finch	-8	272	2	Mike Harwood	Royal Birkdale
1992	Nick Faldo	-12	272	1	John Cook	Muirfield
1993	Greg Norman	-13	267	2	Nick Faldo	Royal St George's
1994	Nick Price	-12	268	1	Jesper Parnevik	Turnberry
1995	John Daly	-6	282	Play-off	Costantino Rocca	St Andrews
1996	Tom Lehman	-13	271	2	Mark McCumber, Ernie Els	Royal Lytham
1997	Justin Leonard	-12	272	3	Jesper Parnevik, Darren Clarke	Royal Troon
1998	Mark O'Meara	E	280	Play-off	Brian Watts	Royal Birkdale
1999	Paul Lawrie	+6	290	Play-off	Justin Leonard, Jean van de Velde	Carnoustie
2000	Tiger Woods	-19	269	8	Ernie Els, Thomas Bjørn	St Andrews
2001	David Duval	-10	274	3	Niclas Fasth	Royal Lytham
2002	Ernie Els	-6	278	Play-off	Thomas Levet, Stuart Appleby, Steve Elkington	Muirfield
2003	Ben Curtis	-1	283	1	Thomas Bjørn, Vijay Singh	Royal St George's
2004	Todd Hamilton	-10	274	Play-off	Ernie Els	Royal Troon
2005	Tiger Woods	-14	274	5	Colin Montgomerie	St Andrews
2006	Tiger Woods	-18	270	2	Chris DiMarco	Royal Liverpool
2007	Padraig Harrington	-7	277	Play-off	Sergio Garcia	Carnoustie
2008	Padraig Harrington	+3	283	4	Ian Poulter	Royal Birkdale
2009	Stewart Cink	-2	278	Play-off	Tom Watson	Turnberry
2010	Louis Oosthuizen	-16	272	7	Lee Westwood	St Andrews
2011	Darren Clarke	-5	275	3	Phil Mickelson, Dustin Johnson	Royal St George's
2012	Ernie Els	-7	273	1	Adam Scott	Royal Lytham
2013	Phil Mickelson	-3	281	3	Henrik Stenson	Muirfield
2014	Rory McIlroy	-17	271	2	Sergio Garcia, Rickie Fowler	Royal Liverpool
2015	Zach Johnson	-15	273	Play-off	Louis Oosthuizen, Marc Leishman	St Andrews
2016	Henrik Stenson	-20	264	3	Phil Mickelson	Royal Troon
2017	Jordan Spieth	-12	268	3	Matt Kuchar	Royal Birkdale
2018	Francesco Molinari	-8	276	2	Justin Rose, Rory McIlroy, Kevin Kisner, Xander Schauffele	Carnoustie
2019	Shane Lowry	-15	269	6	Tommy Fleetwood	Royal Portrush
2020	*No Championship*					
2021	Collin Morikawa	-15	265	2	Jordan Spieth	Royal St George's

Records

Most Victories

6: Harry Vardon, 1896, 1898, 1899, 1903, 1911, 1914
5: James Braid, 1901, 1905, 1906, 1908, 1910; JH Taylor, 1894, 1895, 1900, 1909, 1913; Peter Thomson, 1954, 1955, 1956, 1958, 1965; Tom Watson, 1975, 1977, 1980, 1982, 1983

Most Runner-Up or Joint Runner-Up Finishes

7: Jack Nicklaus, 1964, 1967, 1968, 1972, 1976, 1977, 1979
6: JH Taylor, 1896, 1904, 1905, 1906, 1907, 1914

Oldest Winners

Tom Morris Sr, 1867, 46 years 102 days
Roberto de Vicenzo, 1967, 44 years 92 days
Harry Vardon, 1914, 44 years 41 days
Tom Morris Sr, 1864, 43 years 92 days
Phil Mickelson, 2013, 43 years 35 days
Darren Clarke, 2011, 42 years 337 days
Ernie Els, 2012, 42 years 279 days

Youngest Winners

Tommy Morris Jr, 1868, 17 years 156 days
Tommy Morris Jr, 1869, 18 years 149 days
Tommy Morris Jr, 1870, 19 years 148 days
Willie Auchterlonie, 1893, 21 years 22 days
Tommy Morris Jr, 1872, 21 years 146 days
Seve Ballesteros, 1979, 22 years 103 days

Known Oldest and Youngest Competitors

74 years, 11 months, 24 days: Tom Morris Sr, 1896
74 years, 4 months, 9 days: Gene Sarazen, 1976
14 years, 4 months, 25 days: Tommy Morris Jr, 1865

Largest Margin of Victory

13 strokes, Tom Morris Sr, 1862
12 strokes, Tommy Morris Jr, 1870
11 strokes, Tommy Morris Jr, 1869
8 strokes, JH Taylor, 1900 and 1913; James Braid, 1908; Tiger Woods, 2000

Lowest Winning Total by a Champion

264: Henrik Stenson, Royal Troon, 2016 – 68, 65, 68, 63
265: Collin Morikawa, Royal St George's, 2021 – 67, 64, 68, 66
267: Greg Norman, Royal St George's, 1993 – 66, 68, 69, 64

268: Tom Watson, Turnberry, 1977 – 68, 70, 65, 65; Nick Price, Turnberry, 1994 – 69, 66, 67, 66; Jordan Spieth, Royal Birkdale, 2017 – 65, 69, 65, 69

Lowest Total in Relation to Par Since 1963

20 under par: Henrik Stenson, 2016 (264)
19 under par: Tiger Woods, St Andrews, 2000 (269)
18 under par: Nick Faldo, St Andrews, 1990 (270); Tiger Woods, Royal Liverpool, 2006 (270)

Lowest Total by a Runner-Up

267: Phil Mickelson, Royal Troon, 2016 – 63, 69, 70, 65; Jordan Spieth, Royal St George's, 2021 – 65, 67, 69, 66

Lowest Total by an Amateur

277: Jordan Niebrugge, St Andrews, 2015 – 67, 73, 67, 70

Lowest Individual Round

62: Branden Grace, third round, Royal Birkdale, 2017
63: Mark Hayes, second round, Turnberry, 1977; Isao Aoki, third round, Muirfield, 1980; Greg Norman, second round, Turnberry, 1986; Paul Broadhurst, third round, St Andrews, 1990; Jodie Mudd, fourth round, Royal Birkdale, 1991; Nick Faldo, second round, Royal St George's, 1993; Payne Stewart, fourth round, Royal St George's, 1993; Rory McIlroy, first round, St Andrews, 2010; Phil Mickelson, first round, Royal Troon, 2016; Henrik Stenson, fourth round, Royal Troon, 2016; Haotong Li, fourth round, Royal Birkdale, 2017; Shane Lowry, third round, Royal Portrush, 2019

Lowest Individual Round by an Amateur

65: Tom Lewis, first round, Royal St George's, 2011; Matthias Schmid, second round, Royal St George's, 2021

Lowest First Round

63: Rory McIlroy, St Andrews, 2010; Phil Mickelson, Royal Troon, 2016

Lowest Second Round

63: Mark Hayes, Turnberry, 1977; Greg Norman, Turnberry, 1986; Nick Faldo, Royal St George's, 1993

Lowest Third Round

62: Branden Grace, Royal Birkdale, 2017

Lowest Fourth Round

63: Jodie Mudd, Royal Birkdale, 1991; Payne Stewart, Royal St George's, 1993; Henrik Stenson, Royal Troon, 2016; Haotong Li, Royal Birkdale, 2017

Lowest Score over the First 36 Holes

129: Louis Oosthuizen, Royal St George's, 2021 – 64, 65

Lowest Score over the Middle 36 Holes

130: Fuzzy Zoeller, Turnberry, 1994 – 66, 64; Shane Lowry, Royal Portrush, 2019 – 67, 63

Lowest Score over the Final 36 Holes

130: Tom Watson, Turnberry, 1977 – 65, 65; Ian Baker-Finch, Royal Birkdale, 1991 – 64, 66; Anders Forsbrand, Turnberry, 1994 – 66, 64; Marc Leishman, St Andrews, 2015 – 64, 66

Lowest Score over the First 54 Holes

197: Shane Lowry, Royal Portrush, 2019 – 67, 67, 63
198: Tom Lehman, Royal Lytham & St Annes, 1996 – 67, 67, 64; Louis Oosthuizen, Royal St George's, 2021 – 64, 65, 69

Lowest Score over the Final 54 Holes

196: Henrik Stenson, Royal Troon, 2016 – 65, 68, 63
198: Collin Morikawa, Royal St George's, 2021 – 64, 68, 66; Jon Rahm, Royal St George's, 2021 – 64, 68, 66

Lowest Score for Nine Holes

28: Denis Durnian, first nine, Royal Birkdale, 1983
29: Tom Haliburton, first nine, Royal Lytham & St Annes, 1963; Peter Thomson, first nine, Royal Lytham & St Annes, 1963; Tony Jacklin, first nine, St Andrews, 1970; Bill Longmuir, first nine, Royal Lytham & St Annes, 1979; David J Russell first nine, Royal Lytham & St Annes, 1988; Ian Baker-Finch, first nine, St Andrews, 1990; Paul Broadhurst, first nine, St Andrews, 1990; Ian Baker-Finch, first nine, Royal Birkdale, 1991; Paul McGinley, first nine, Royal Lytham & St Annes, 1996; Ernie Els, first nine, Muirfield, 2002; Sergio Garcia, first nine, Royal Liverpool, 2006; David Lingmerth, first nine, St Andrews, 2015; Matt Kuchar, first nine, Royal Birkdale, 2017; Branden Grace, first nine, Royal Birkdale, 2017; Ryan Fox, second nine, Royal Portrush, 2019

Most Successive Victories

4: Tommy Morris Jr, 1868-72 (No Championship in 1871)
3: Jamie Anderson, 1877-79; Bob Ferguson, 1880-82; Peter Thomson, 1954-56
2: Tom Morris Sr, 1861-62; JH Taylor, 1894-95; Harry Vardon, 1898-99; James Braid, 1905-06; Bobby Jones, 1926-27; Walter Hagen, 1928-29; Bobby Locke, 1949-50; Arnold Palmer, 1961-62; Lee Trevino, 1971-72; Tom Watson, 1982-83; Tiger Woods, 2005-06; Padraig Harrington, 2007-08

Amateurs Who Have Won The Open

3: Bobby Jones, Royal Lytham & St Annes, 1926; St Andrews, 1927; Royal Liverpool, 1930
2: Harold Hilton, Muirfield, 1892; Royal Liverpool, 1897
1: John Ball Jr, Prestwick, 1890

Champions Who Won on Debut

Willie Park Sr, Prestwick, 1860; Tom Kidd, St Andrews, 1873; Mungo Park, Musselburgh, 1874; Jock Hutchison, St Andrews, 1921; Denny Shute, St Andrews, 1933; Ben Hogan, Carnoustie, 1953; Tony Lema, St Andrews, 1964; Tom Watson, Carnoustie, 1975; Ben Curtis, Royal St George's, 2003; Collin Morikawa, Royal St George's, 2021

Attendance

Year	Total
1960	39,563
1961	21,708
1962	37,098
1963	24,585
1964	35,954
1965	32,927
1966	40,182
1967	29,880
1968	51,819
1969	46,001
1970	81,593
1971	70,076
1972	84,746
1973	78,810
1974	92,796
1975	85,258
1976	92,021
1977	87,615
1978	125,271
1979	134,501
1980	131,610
1981	111,987
1982	133,299
1983	142,892
1984	193,126
1985	141,619
1986	134,261
1987	139,189
1988	191,334
1989	160,639
1990	208,680
1991	189,435
1992	146,427
1993	141,000
1994	128,000
1995	180,000
1996	170,000
1997	176,000
1998	195,100
1999	157,000
2000	239,000
2001	178,000
2002	161,500
2003	183,000
2004	176,000
2005	223,000
2006	230,000
2007	154,000
2008	201,500
2009	123,000
2010	201,000
2011	180,100
2012	181,300
2013	142,036
2014	202,917
2015	237,024
2016	173,134
2017	235,000
2018	172,000
2019	237,750
2021	152,330

Greatest Interval Between First and Last Victory

19 years: JH Taylor, 1894-1913
18 years: Harry Vardon, 1896-1914
15 years: Willie Park Sr, 1860-75; Gary Player, 1959-74
14 years: Henry Cotton, 1934-48

Greatest Interval Between Victories

11 years: Henry Cotton, 1937-48 (No Championship 1940-45)
10 years: Ernie Els, 2002-12
9 years: Willie Park Sr, 1866-75; Bob Martin, 1876-85; JH Taylor, 1900-09; Gary Player, 1959-68

Champions Who Have Won in Three Separate Decades

Harry Vardon, 1896, 1898 & 1899/1903/1911 & 1914
JH Taylor, 1894 & 1895/1900 & 1909/1913
Gary Player, 1959/1968/1974

Competitors with the Most Top Five Finishes

16: JH Taylor; Jack Nicklaus

Competitors Who Have Recorded the Most Rounds Under Par From 1963

59: Jack Nicklaus
54: Nick Faldo
53: Ernie Els

Competitors with the Most Finishes Under Par From 1963

15: Ernie Els
14: Jack Nicklaus; Nick Faldo
13: Tom Watson

Champions Who Have Led Outright After Every Round

72 hole Championships
Ted Ray, 1912; Bobby Jones, 1927; Gene Sarazen, 1932; Henry Cotton, 1934; Tom Weiskopf, 1973; Tiger Woods, 2005; Rory McIlroy, 2014
36 hole Championships
Willie Park Sr, 1860 and 1866; Tom Morris Sr, 1862 and 1864; Tommy Morris Jr, 1869 and 1870; Mungo Park, 1874; Jamie Anderson, 1879; Bob Ferguson, 1880, 1881, 1882; Willie Fernie, 1883; Jack Simpson, 1884; Hugh Kirkaldy, 1891

Largest Leads Since 1892

After 18 holes:
5 strokes: Sandy Herd, 1896
4 strokes: Harry Vardon, 1902; Jim Barnes, 1925; Christy O'Connor Jr, 1985
After 36 holes:
9 strokes: Henry Cotton, 1934
6 strokes: Abe Mitchell, 1920
After 54 holes:
10 strokes: Henry Cotton, 1934
7 strokes: Harry Vardon, 1903; Tony Lema, 1964
6 strokes: JH Taylor, 1900; James Braid, 1905; James Braid, 1908; Max Faulkner, 1951; Tom Lehman, 1996; Tiger Woods, 2000; Rory McIlroy, 2014

Champions Who Had Four Rounds, Each Better than the One Before

Jack White, Royal St George's, 1904 – 80, 75, 72, 69
James Braid, Muirfield, 1906 – 77, 76, 74, 73
Ben Hogan, Carnoustie, 1953 – 73, 71, 70, 68
Gary Player, Muirfield, 1959 – 75, 71, 70, 68

Same Number of Strokes in Each of the Four Rounds by a Champion

Denny Shute, St Andrews, 1933 – 73, 73, 73, 73 (excluding the play-off)

Best 18-Hole Recovery by a Champion

George Duncan, Deal, 1920. Duncan was 13 strokes behind the leader, Abe Mitchell, after 36 holes and level with him after 54.

Greatest Variation Between Rounds by a Champion

14 strokes: Henry Cotton, 1934, second round 65, fourth round 79
12 strokes: Henry Cotton, 1934, first round 67, fourth round 79
11 strokes: Jack White, 1904, first round 80, fourth round 69; Greg Norman, 1986, first round 74, second round 63; Greg Norman, 1986, second round 63, third round 74
10 strokes: Seve Ballesteros, 1979, second round 65, third round 75

Greatest Variation Between Two Successive Rounds by a Champion

11 strokes: Greg Norman, 1986, first round 74, second round 63; Greg Norman, 1986, second round 63, third round 74

Greatest Comeback by a Champion

After 18 holes
Harry Vardon, 1896, 11 strokes behind the leader
After 36 holes
George Duncan, 1920, 13 strokes behind the leader
After 54 holes
Paul Lawrie, 1999, 10 strokes behind the leader

Champions Who Had Four Rounds Under 70

Greg Norman, Royal St George's, 1993 – 66, 68, 69, 64; Nick Price, Turnberry, 1994 – 69, 66, 67, 66; Tiger Woods, St Andrews, 2000 – 67, 66, 67, 69; Henrik Stenson, Royal Troon, 2016 – 68, 65, 68, 63; Jordan Spieth, Royal Birkdale, 2017 – 65, 69, 65, 69; Collin Morikawa, Royal St George's, 2021 – 67, 64, 68, 66

Competitors Who Failed to Win The Open Despite Having Four Rounds Under 70

Ernie Els, Royal St George's, 1993 – 68, 69, 69, 68; Jesper Parnevik, Turnberry, 1994 – 68, 66, 68, 67; Ernie Els, Royal Troon, 2004 – 69, 69, 68, 68; Rickie Fowler, Royal Liverpool, 2014 – 69, 69, 68, 67; Jordan Spieth, Royal St George's, 2021 – 65, 67, 69, 66; Mackenzie Hughes, Royal St George's, 2021 – 66, 69, 68, 69

Lowest Final Round by a Champion

63: Henrik Stenson, Royal Troon, 2016
64: Greg Norman, Royal St George's, 1993
65: Tom Watson, Turnberry, 1977; Seve Ballesteros, Royal Lytham & St Annes, 1988; Justin Leonard, Royal Troon, 1997

Worst Round by a Champion Since 1939

78: Fred Daly, third round, Royal Liverpool,
77: Dick Burton, third round, St Andrews, 1939
76: Bobby Locke, second round, Royal St George's, 1949; Paul Lawrie, third round, Carnoustie, 1999

Champion with the Worst Finishing Round Since 1939

75: Sam Snead, St Andrews, 1946

Lowest Opening Round by a Champion

65: Louis Oosthuizen, St Andrews, 2010; Jordan Spieth, Royal Birkdale, 2017

Most Open Championship Appearances

46: Gary Player
43: Sandy Lyle
38: Sandy Herd, Jack Nicklaus, Tom Watson
37: Nick Faldo

Most Final Day Appearances Since 1892

32: Jack Nicklaus
31: Sandy Herd
30: JH Taylor
28: Ted Ray
27: Harry Vardon, James Braid, Nick Faldo
26: Peter Thomson, Gary Player, Tom Watson

Most Appearances by a Champion Before His First Victory

19: Darren Clarke, 2011; Phil Mickelson, 2013
15: Nick Price, 1994
14: Sandy Herd, 1902
13: Ted Ray, 1912; Jack White, 1904; Reg Whitcombe, 1938; Mark O'Meara, 1998
11: George Duncan, 1920; Nick Faldo, 1987; Ernie Els, 2002; Stewart Cink, 2009; Zach Johnson, 2015; Henrik Stenson, 2016

The Open Which Provided the Greatest Number of Rounds Under 70 Since 1946

169 rounds, Royal St George's, 2021

The Open with the Fewest Rounds Under 70 Since 1946

2 rounds, St Andrews, 1946; Royal Liverpool, 1947; Carnoustie, 1968

Statistically Most Difficult Hole Since 1982

St Andrews, 1984, Par-4 17th, 4.79

Longest Course in Open History

Carnoustie, 2007, 7,421 yards

Number of Times Each Course Has Hosted The Open

St Andrews, 29; Prestwick, 24; Muirfield, 16; Royal St George's, 15; Royal Liverpool, 12; Royal Lytham & St Annes, 11; Royal Birkdale, 10; Royal Troon, 9; Carnoustie, 8; Musselburgh, 6; Turnberry, 4; Royal Cinque Ports, 2; Royal Portrush, 2; Prince's, 1

Increases in Prize Money (£)

Year	Total	First Prize	Year	Total	First Prize	Year	Total	First Prize	Year	Total	First Prize
1860	nil	nil	1891	28.50	10	1969	30,000	4,250	1996	1,400,000	200,000
1863	10	nil	1892	110	35	1970	40,000	5,250	1997	1,600,000	250,000
1864	15	6	1893	100	30	1971	45,000	5,500	1998	1,800,000	300,000
1865	20	8	1900	125	50	1972	50,000	5,500	1999	2,000,000	350,000
1866	11	6	1910	135	50	1975	75,000	7,500	2000	2,750,000	500,000
1867	16	7	1920	225	75	1977	100,000	10,000	2001	3,300,000	600,000
1868	12	6	1927	275	75	1978	125,000	12,500	2002	3,800,000	700,000
1872	unknown	8	1930	400	100	1979	155,000	15,000	2003	3,900,000	700,000
1873	unknown	11	1931	500	100	1980	200,000	25,000	2004	4,000,000	720,000
1874	20	8	1946	1,000	150	1982	250,000	32,000	2007	4,200,000	750,000
1876	27	10	1949	1,500	300	1983	310,000	40,000	2010	4,800,000	850,000
1877	20	8	1951	1,700	300	1984	451,000	55,000	2011	5,000,000	900,000
1878	unknown	8	1953	2,500	500	1985	530,000	65,000	2013	5,250,000	945,000
1879	47	10	1954	3,500	750	1986	600,000	70,000	2014	5,400,000	975,000
1880	unknown	8	1955	3,750	1,000	1987	650,000	75,000	2015	6,300,000	1,150,000
1881	21	8	1958	4,850	1,000	1988	700,000	80,000	2016	6,500,000	1,175,000
1882	47.25	12	1959	5,000	1,000	1989	750,000	80,000	2017	$10,250,000	$1,845,000
1883	20	8	1960	7,000	1,250	1990	825,000	85,000	2018	$10,500,000	$1,890,000
1884	23	8	1961	8,500	1,400	1991	900,000	90,000	2019	$10,750,000	$1,935,000
1885	35.50	10	1963	8,500	1,500	1992	950,000	95,000	2021	$11,500,000	$2,070,000
1886	20	8	1965	10,000	1,750	1993	1,000,000	100,000			
1889	22	8	1966	15,000	2,100	1994	1,100,000	110,000			
1890	29.50	13	1968	20,000	3,000	1995	1,250,000	125,000			

PHOTOGRAPHY CREDITS

David Cannon – 1, 19, 24 bottom, 46 bottom, 55 bottom, 57 top, 60, 85, 90 bottom, 92 top left, 99, 103, 106, 121 right, 123 left, 128 bottom left & right.

Harry Trump – 4, 23, 32, 38 top, 58, 62, 66, 76 top, 81 top, 88 left, 91 bottom left, 101 left, 104.

Oisin Keniry – 6, 16, 18 top, 30 top, 35, 38 bottom right, 42, 51 bottom, 63, 92 bottom, 93 bottom, 95 top.

Tom Shaw – 12, 20 top, 24 top, 38 bottom left, 54 bottom, 56 left & right, 74 bottom left, 76 bottom, 128 top left.

Christopher Lee – 10, 28, 46 top, 51 top, 57 bottom, 86 top, 89 bottom.

Stephen Pond – 14 top, 20 inset, 21, 40 bottom, 68 top, 71, 72, 74 top, 76 bottom right, 92 top right.

Warren Little – 14 bottom, 18 bottom, 36 top, 40 top, 50, 52, 68 bottom, 71 bottom, 75, 94, 95 bottom, 97, 98, 128 top right.

Mike Hewitt – 15, 31, 43 inset, 48, 80, 91 bottom right.

Andrew Redington – 25, 34 bottom, 37, 39, 54 top, 77, 77 inset, 82, 84, 86 bottom, 101 right, 123 centre.

Chris Trotman – 26, 30 bottom, 36 bottom, 87, 90 top, 91 top.

Charlie Crowhurst – 34 top, 44, 47, 55 top, 69, 70 top & bottom, 78, 93 bottom.

Matthew Lewis – 43 top, 64, 88 right, 89 top.

Stuart Franklin – 81 bottom.

Other pictures courtesy of The R&A and Getty Images.

ROYAL ST GEORGE'S

THE 149TH OPEN
CARD OF THE CHAMPIONSHIP COURSE

HOLE	PAR	YARDS	HOLE	PAR	YARDS
1	4	445	10	4	415
2	4	421	11	3	238
3	3	239	12	4	379
4	4	491	13	4	456
5	4	422	14	5	547
6	3	174	15	4	496
7	5	566	16	3	162
8	4	450	17	4	426
9	4	412	18	4	450
OUT	**35**	**3,620**	**IN**	**35**	**3,569**
			TOTAL	**70**	**7,189**